OWN

—— THE ——

MOMENT

Carl Lentz

Simon & Schuster

New York   London   Toronto   Sydney   New Delhi

Simon & Schuster
1230 Avenue of the Americas
New York, NY 10020

First Simon & Schuster hardcover edition October 2017

SIMON & SCHUSTER and colophon are registered
trademarks of Simon & Schuster, Inc.

For information about special discounts for bulk purchases, please contact
Simon & Schuster Special Sales at 1-866-506-1949
or business@simonandschuster.com.

The Simon & Schuster Speakers Bureau can bring authors to your live event.
For more information or to book an event, contact the
Simon & Schuster Speakers Bureau at 1-866-248-3049 or
visit our website at www.simonspeakers.com.

Interior design by Ruth Lee-Mui
Endpaper photograph by Jordann Wood/Hillsong Church NYC

Manufactured in the United States of America

1   3   5   7   9   10   8   6   4   2

Library of Congress Cataloging-in-Publication Data has been applied for.

ISBN 978-1-5011-7700-2
ISBN 978-1-5011-7701-9 (ebook)

This book is dedicated to the four people to who I can honestly say, "I loved you from the moment I saw you."

Laura Jayne Lentz, I'm forever grateful to God that I get to be your husband. People find it hard to believe when I tell them that I honestly knew I was going to marry you from the moment I saw you. I called my mom that day in Australia, and said, "Mom, I saw the woman I'm gonna marry today." Thankfully, Cathy Lentz can verify this, and it's a moment that I'm glad I will never forget. You're a better human being than I am, your relationship with Jesus inspires me to dig deeper into my own soul and grow daily, and the way you give grace to people is unmatched. Grace to forgive. Grace to take what life throws at us and make it work. Grace to let me continually find my stride as a man, a dad, a husband, a friend without judgment or doubt. I could and should write a whole book about you. Maybe I will one day. But thanks for sticking with me this long—long enough to actually have enough to say to write a book at all! I would have given up on all this many, many times along the road. But each time you wouldn't let that be an option. I'm thankful for that. You are my best friend, you are easy to love, and you have my whole heart forever. I love you!

To Ava Angel Lentz, Charlie Jayne Lentz, and Roman Stephen (and sometimes Roger) Lentz: There are no words that can articulate how much I love you.

Ava, thanks for letting me tell lame dad jokes in front of your friends and allowing me to drive you to school and stay far too long as I always ask to watch you walk *all* the way in because I just can't get enough of you. Please ask God to slow down your growth process. The only thing growing faster than your legs is your passion to know more about God—and your grace and class that already set you apart from everybody. May you carry that grace and class the rest of your life.

Charlie Jayne, you have made us smile from the moment you took a breath on this Earth, and I love your deep soul that cares so much for people and how they feel. It's so rare and I'm dedicated to protecting that the rest of your life. You make people feel special, and that is a gift from God. I'm proud to be your daddy!

And to my son, Roman the Lion: You are a world changer. You are a legend. You are a man of God, and you are called and anointed to do great things on this Earth. I'm going to do all I can to carve out a path for you to follow that leads to a life of significant impact. Being your dad has already made me a better man. You're my guy, my buddy, and I'm proud of you.

Thank you, Lentz family, for the dinners missed, the preoccupied bike rides, and the vacant stares it cost you as I gave this book all I had. I know it will be worth it. It's a blessing to get to spend this life with the four of you.

Contents

Contents

Disclaimers

I WROTE THIS BOOK. All of it. I don't say that to boast, because being an author is not something I ever thought I would be. But as I learned about the process, and some of the ins and outs of the business side of things, I found out what is common, what is unique, what is standard procedure for writing books these days. And this is not exposing anything new or meant to be even remotely disparaging. It's just true: A lot of authors don't write a lot of their own books. First, because it's smart. Writing effectively is extremely difficult. And if the goal is to get your book to help as many people as possible, it makes sense to use every single tool at your disposal—including an editor who is most likely a professional who can transcribe or translate what's in your heart, on paper, better than you could. Most of the time people choose that option. I don't blame them—and at times I wished I had too! But I chose to roll the dice with this book, and make sure it's my voice, my heart, my passion, for better or worse—perhaps to its detriment, professionally speaking. But I've never done things according to the professional, cultural norm. And I don't intend to start now. So if this book seems unorthodox, unpolished, different, up and down, long chapters and shorter chapters, and in some spots even incomplete? That's because it is. In some ways, that's exactly how it should be. This book was written in a black Chevy Tahoe on the streets of Brooklyn, NYC. This book was written in the slums of Mumbai, India. This book was written over vast, aqua-blue, endless ocean water, flying to various places in this amazing world. It was written at my kitchen table in Montclair, New Jersey. It was written in a hospital waiting room while a friend was in surgery. It was written through tears, throughout its entirety. And in some strange way, I'm really comfortable with that. Because for me to tell you to "own your moment," and not be truly real and transparent in my moment to write this book would make no sense. I pray it's a blessing in your life. I wrote this the way I would want to read it. Over the years I learned that I don't really like to read books that often because my attention span is so sporadic. Sometimes I can sit for a long time and read.

Other times, reading three tweets is all my mind can digest. So I thought if I ever did write a book, I would include both. Long chapters and short ones. Just to make sure everybody is covered. I also have a tendency to pick up books in random spots. This is a problem if a book has to be read chronologically to fully understand it. This book is not like that. You can pick it up in any chapter, any time, and that chapter will make sense on its own. In summary, all you fellow ADHD people? This book is for you. Thank you for spending your money to buy it. It's an overwhelming honor to have even a moment to offer some perspective into your life. As my man Charlamagne tha God says, "I will hold my tongue for no one." And if that means putting it on paper for the world to read, critique, love, and hate? It is what it is. I'm gonna own my moments. I have a feeling this book will help you own yours too.

I am going to use a whole lot of real-life, real-time stories that include actual real people. Because without them, this becomes a book of ideas. I don't know about you, but as much as I love ideas, I want to know that something somebody is proposing actually works. Due to the personal nature of my life and the people who trust me, sometimes I will change a name or characteristic, or give a more vague description of a matter. But the stories that I use are real.

I am an out-of-the-closet, flamboyantly outspoken follower of Jesus. This matters, because every single thing I do or say or write comes directly through the lens of my faith. Which is solely and completely rooted in Jesus Christ. This is not my religion. This is my relationship with God. Huge difference. If you read this book, you do not have to believe what I believe. The stone-cold truth about Jesus and what He stood for and stands for is that you don't actually have to believe He was who He said He was and who I say He is to benefit from His life. In fact, most successful "motivational speakers" simply rip off Bible teaching—they take the Bible out of it, give no credit to the author, and make a killing. What I found out is that, yes, doing what Jesus said to do can change your life on this Earth. It can change your behavior and your outlook. But that's not why Jesus came to this Earth. He did not come to be a nice addition and to "make your life better." He is salvation. He is the prize. He is the answer. He claimed to be God, and I believe He is. I follow Jesus because He saved my life and has given me a new life, and He is the only one that can change our eternal destination. So you can still read this and adhere to what you believe. But you have to understand that the thing that makes me "different" is God's grace. Yes, I work hard. Yes, I have implemented principles that have truly helped me make an impact thus far in my life. But I know a lot of people who work hard—work harder, in fact. I know a lot of people who have diligently put time, effort, and passion into various things in their lives, and the outcome is much different. The truth is, we don't always know what it is that becomes the "decider" in our lives. Be careful when you see people say, "If you do this right here? This right here will be your outcome." No way. This life is a blink. It's a vapor. So what we believe at our core truly matters. I won't be "forcing my faith" on you throughout this book. Actually, quite the opposite. This isn't a "Christian book." After all, what does that even mean? I don't think I have ever seen any other faith-based category so marginalized. I've never seen "Read this book by this guy. He is a cow-worshipping author." Or, "See what this guy from the hip-hop world has to say. He is a self-worshipping author." Only Christians get hit with that brush. So don't do that. But also be aware that my faith in Jesus is the only congruent thread in the fabric of my entire life. You believe what you need to believe. I'll believe what I need to believe. And even if it's different, I think you will find we agree on many important things. Read this with an open mind, and I do think it can open some doors for you.

I will include, when necessary, stories about people who some deem "famous." The fact that these people are famous holds very little weight with me. I love people regardless of status. However, in our culture, "celebrity currency" reaches far and wide. Celebrity currency is the idea that fame means value. I disagree with this. I think fame *can* mean influence, but it's common now to be famous for simply being well-known and not because an individual has made a positive impact on anybody or anything. Regardless, the names of famous people and the association with fame itself is exactly how stories gain traction, how clubs get put on the map, and cheap status gets placed on something. I'm excited to use that same logic to point to something redemptive and meaningful. I get asked about famous people very frequently, and normally I don't give a lot of comment or context about it because I don't have the time to do so. I do here. Our church in NYC is probably 99.9 percent full of nonfamous people. The media has never once asked to do a story on people they do not know and how awesome they are. So often, we hear terms like "celebrity church." It's a false narrative. But that's the thing: It's somebody else's narrative. The big advantage of writing a book is that we get to shed light accurately on this one aspect that brings a whole lot of attention. That's why I have included stories about people you may have heard about—because they add perspective to a much bigger picture. But I don't think this adds worth to *my* value. I'm thirty-eight years old. My wife, Laura, is fantastically gorgeous, and she is madly in love with me. (When I say "madly," please note that we have three children and all of them have a birthday in the first two weeks of June. She is apparently crazy for me, especially in October. Hello!) And my kids (for the time being) think that I am awesome. Those factors make up my self-worth equation. So I am completely secure in my coolness without ever knowing a famous person or being linked to a famous person or telling stories about them. However, I would be remiss not to redeem the shallow attraction that is fame if I didn't show how it can still be a light in some sort of situation.

OWN
— THE —
MOMENT

Introduction

OWN THE MOMENT. The concept seems simple enough. There are literally millions upon millions of moments in our lives that we will either maximize or that we will miss. Whether we are more efficient with the former or the latter has a huge impact on what the final picture of our lives will ultimately look like.

I have never been a big "puzzle guy." And by that I mean I *despise* puzzles. But when you have children, you have to put up with some pain, like watching them slowly piece together what will at some point or some year—depending on the attention span of said child—turn out to be a picture. Some pieces are small, and some pieces are larger, and you can skip one or two if you feel like it, but at the end it will look like it's missing something. Worse yet, you can sit there and look at all the pieces and expect or hope that somebody, someday, is going to come make sense of all this and put it together for you.

I think our culture—which is built on quick gratification, shortcuts to success, filming events we are actually at so we can record them to watch later if ever, and a victim currency that is so robust that when things don't happen that we like or want it's rarely our fault—is setting us up for the ultimate hustle. Which is to be in this life but never actually *live it*. To be present in body but absent in mind. To live and breathe achievement and success and accomplishment, to continually gather these things only to find out they were not what they were advertised to be.

You know what my goal is? I want to own the moments in my life. I want to, yes, take a photo of my son riding his bike . . . but I also want to put my phone away and actually see him do it. Yes, I want to work hard and save money and make sure my children leave my house someday and walk into a setup that will help them win in every way. But I don't want them to walk out of my house total strangers because I was so intent on working for their future that I missed their present.

I believe in this book, with my entire being. Because it's not always life or death when you miss a moment. If you hesitated to ask somebody out that you like, and somebody else owned the moment and you are still single? There will be more moments, relax. If you missed an anniversary and remembered a day later and your spouse said, "Thanks but no thanks," you may have to get acquainted with your couch for a little while, but you can make next year's anniversary count. Missing moments happens to us all. My greater concern in my own life, and for anybody who picks up this book, is that if you build a pattern of missing moments that don't appear to be significant, you will miss out on what builds a life that leads to many huge moments, connections, relationships, and experiences. And some moments? You'd better believe they are life and death.

Our first few years in NYC planting this amazing church were very much like a whirlwind. We didn't have a lot of experience,[1] but we had a lot of passion. And the people and the pace that make up NYC require every bit of passion you can muster up. Learning how to own the moment can be the difference between a taxi you do or don't get, a sliver of space on a subway that you have to be on, a mix tape or a movie script or a business idea that you just had to share. Because in NYC? You run into difference makers everywhere you go. Split seconds

---

[1]Actually, *none.*

can equate to multi-millions. When it comes to other people, owning the moment can also mean saving a life. Since we have no idea what somebody else might be going through, taking a moment to say hi, send an encouraging text, make an extra phone call just to let somebody know they are loved could be everything to an individual. Moments matter.

Two of my best friends and I had been working with a friend who some would say was "vintage NYC." He was a model, a clothing designer, and made some really good decisions in the stock market that enabled him to have and spend a lot of money. I don't know how many businesses he owned, but I am aware of how many millions of dollars he spent on things that didn't really matter. So let's just say he was very, very good at what he did. He also had a wicked cocaine and heroin addiction that had shadowed him for almost twenty years. I had heard of "functioning addicts" before I got to NYC, but I always pictured people from the movie *Joe Dirt* in some backwater town that was just barely getting by. Little did I know that not only could you function while being highly addicted to deadly narcotics, you could in fact still thrive in some areas.

My friend was clean for a solid five months, but I noticed some odd things over the course of two weeks that made me concerned. I checked with my two friends, who loved this person as much as me, and none of us had heard from him that whole period of time. When this guy is clicking on all cylinders, he's a ten-texts-a-day type of guy. So the difference is stark. We all landed on the same conclusion: He was most likely bunkered away in his gorgeous penthouse apartment, on a binge. This is problematic because when this happens with addicts, you never know if this will be the one that takes them out completely. They don't know either. But after two or three days of mainlining heroin, you tend to lose your logic.

We went to his apartment, and we could hear noise, so we knew he was in there. I called his phone. I could hear it ring. And he picked it up and said, "I'm not here." I started beating on the door, saying, "I can hear, my brother. Open this door up. I love you. I just want to talk to you." That was a lie, and he knew it was a lie, because I wasn't going to talk to him. I was going to ask once if he wanted to go to rehab. And if the answer was no, I was going to punch him in the face and drag him out. He and I had been together in this situation before, only he was on the other side of the door with me. So he knew better.

We knocked for a while, reasoned with him, and realized it was hopeless. We thought we had a moment, we did what we could, and dejection set in. And then another moment presented itself. My friend Joe—who is as relentless about his friends and people in general as anybody I have ever known—said, "You know what? Screw this. He's not dying tonight." His brother John—who is equally insane when it comes to never giving up on anything—said, "Yeah, I'm with you." Joe said, "We can climb that fire escape. John, I can hang there and pull you up, and then you can get on my shoulders, and we can throw this cinderblock through his giant bay window. And Carl, we will open the door for you and the three of us can drag him out."

Sometimes you are faced with moments in life that literally scare you to death. But if what you love or believe matters enough? You will own it. So we reluctantly, together, owned this moment, huddled like a football team, prayed that police would not see us and arrest us, and that none of us would die. You know, the essentials. And the two brothers went to work.

It was exactly like a scene out of a movie. Joe somehow climbed up the fire escape. He hung his arm down, and John was almost catapulted up by him.[2] The cinderblock was by the window, and I gave my friend one more chance.

"Bro, please. Open the door. Trust me."

"I won't! Leave me alone! I don't want help!"

I gave Joe the thumbs-up, and next thing you heard was glass breaking, a bit of a tussle, and the front door flew open. Joe had my friend in a very loving headlock-hug. John was out of breath. My friend had given up at this point.

"I'll go," he said.

---

[2] I do believe this was not the first time either of these boys had done something like this.

My friend lived to see another day, to fight that hellacious addiction for at least a few more rounds.

———————————

When I think back to that scene, I love the memory. I love all the factors involved. But my mind lands back on Joe. He felt faith for a fleeting moment and *owned* that moment. And it led to a few more moments, which now, as we look back on them, are an epic memory that will stay with me forever. But that puzzle didn't just come together. It was pieced together.

I wrote this book because I don't care who you are, what you do, or how good or bad it may seem today: I know we can all do a better job of making the most of what we do have. Focusing on what we *can* do. Maybe, just maybe, there is a cinderblock lying around somewhere that you can throw through the glass barriers that surround your life. It won't happen right away, but the process can begin whenever you want it to. Day by day. Step by step. Choice by choice. Piece by piece. If you own what's right in front of you, I do believe that someday, when you sit down to tell the story of your life, it's going to take a while. Because you have so many moments that deserve their own microphone.

Chapter One

Surprise! What You See Is Not What You Get

THROUGHOUT MY ENTIRE LIFE, I have ended up in situations that surprise me. Places that in some ways I'm not qualified for. Open doors that I didn't ask for. Moments that clearly are much greater than my natural capacity calls for. Yet there I was, here I am, and most likely there I will be.

In the deep end.

I'm okay with this, because one thing I do not want said of me someday is: "Hey, that guy Carl Lentz? He lived up to his potential." What a shame that would be. Potential is great, and I speak about it often. But in no way do I want my "potential" to run congruent with my life path. I want to keep doing things that obviously don't compute with what I'm naturally able to do. My current "occupation"—pastor of a local church—is a bright and shining example of this.

———————————

I grew up in a family that was not perfect but pretty close. My mom and dad have been married for close to fifty years, and I have watched them love each other sacrificially and faithfully, every day of my life. I have three sisters who are all spectacular in their own ways. Although distance has made contact and regular communication more challenging as we have all grown up and stepped out in life, they have always been and will always be my three best friends. Mary, Bethany, and Corrie have always had my back and been my biggest supporters, at every stage of my random life.

There is a photo that definitely represents my childhood growing up as the only boy in a house with four women. I have a cowboy hat on, a Western shirt, a holster with two toy six-shooters, jeans . . . and high heels. I was probably about six, but evidently I blindly trusted whichever sister thought *This will be funny when he gets older.* I just rolled with it. Whatever. We all have photos like that.

Our family dynamic was rooted in a relationship with Jesus. Not a "religious family" but one that had a real, live, active faith. The difference is that religion is almost always passed down and accepted as fact. My parents raised us to search out truth for ourselves. Even now, when I ask people why they believe what they believe, often the response is "Well, my mother said . . ." Or, "The church I grew up in believes . . ." To which I say, "Not good enough." At some point, people have to choose what *they* believe. My parents did this so well that I was allowed to even walk away from my faith at one point. They trusted truth would win out, and it did.

But for a while I chose to take a different route. I loved basketball, poured my life into it, and that basically became everything to me. I was present in high school just enough to keep my grades high enough to play more basketball. I was good, which was surprising. I'm 6'2" and not particularly athletic, but I learned quickly that if you work hard enough and you have even decent skills, you can get pretty far. In everything.

With my average skill set, I made it to the pinnacle of college basketball, the vaunted Atlantic Coast Conference, the ACC, and somehow landed a spot on the North Carolina State basketball team. I remember playing UNC, playing Duke at Cameron Indoor Stadium—places that I had previously seen as fantasy lands—and thinking, *I can't believe I am here.* I'm positive that anybody who saw me on this team was thinking the same thing. But I was there.

This became my pattern for life. When I went to Bible college after making the choice to leave conventional study and pursue my faith, the same thing happened in Australia. Brian Houston saw something in me as a very raw,[1] outspoken, and passionate young Bible college student, and chose to help me. To lead me. To teach me.

Brian is the global senior pastor of Hillsong Church and, in my opinion, perhaps the most significant local church pastor in a very, very long time. A lot of what is commonplace in churches now, Brian did first. Things like multi-campus interaction; multi-site vision for a congregation that works together, not autonomously; and in general a preaching style that is so practical and inspiring, you don't want to leave church when it finishes.[2] Brian was one of a few brave leaders to earnestly try new things to reach people. So for him to care about me at all? A surprise.

But perhaps the icing on the "I shouldn't be here" cake would be the fact that I am a preacher. A public speaker. When I made the choice to pursue my relationship with Jesus, I said, "God, I will do anything You ask. Except be a preacher." Famous last words, to be sure. I just figured that I'm lucky to be alive. Never in my life had I spoken publicly, nor remotely desired to speak publicly, and I knew that preachers and speakers

---

[1] Still am.
[2] Many of us have been in those services where we whisper quietly to Heaven, "Please, God, make it stop."

were open targets for people to take shots at. I was also aware I simply didn't have that gift set. Although I had defied my "natural ability" my whole life, I thought at some point I needed to get "realistic" and aim a bit lower perhaps. God, however—as I have come to learn all too well—is not all that interested in our idea of our own potential. Regardless how hard you try to hide.

———————

I showed up at Bible college one day in full possession of my books, my potential, and my fear and loathing of public speaking, just like I did every day. Only this was not an ordinary day; it was a day that changed the entire course of my life. We had a chapel service every Tuesday, and I loved it. Music was played, somebody would get up and preach, and we would go about our day. But on this day, a man named Phil Dooley—who is now the pastor of Hillsong South Africa and is simply one of the most encouraging, loving, and hilarious mentors I have ever had—got up and said, "Today we are going to pray for different countries in need. I'm going to ask different students to get up here and pray for their country." He started calling names: "Thomas from Denmark, get up here. Nick from Australia, get up here." My stomach dropped as he continued this Death Roll Call, and sure enough: "Carl from the USA, get up here and pray for your country."

The moment I heard my name, I went from the front of the room to shifting through the crowd like I had stolen something. I then broke into a full sprint, ran out of the room, and went to hide. The first option I saw was the bathroom, and I took it. I doubled down on my hiding spot, shut the bathroom stall door, closed the toilet seat, and stood on it to ensure no trace would be evident that I was in that room. I think I stayed in there for about forty-five minutes. And for a moment—huddled in a bathroom stall, hiding out of fear, on the literal opposite side of planet Earth from where I was born, after all I had been through thus far—I considered my present situation. Here I was, a person who had already made major choices to step out in faith that had led to me defying almost every bit of meager potential that I felt I had, hiding because I was scared to do something I didn't think I was capable of doing. I shook my head, shut my eyes, and prayed something that at times I regret. But more times I thank God that I did: "From here on out, Jesus, if You open the door, I'm going to walk through it. I don't care if I look stupid. I don't care if I don't think I'm capable of it. You did not save my life for me to hide out in a bathroom stall because I'm scared. This is my pledge, starting now."

That day, I left some of my fear, some of my hesitation, and some of my introspective self-judgment. I say "some" because there is not a single human on Earth who has completely overcome every identity and security challenge that comes with being inherently imperfect. But I left *all* of my potential behind that day. Because since then? More than ever, I keep surprising people. I keep surprising *myself*. Through prayer, trial and error, surrounding myself with people who are better than me in so many areas, I am an example of what God can do with somebody who is not amazing but *available*. Open to being used. Interested in being challenged. Resigned to living a life that is continually out of my comfort zone. It's not easy, it's just better.

———————

I think the only person not surprised was Cathy Lentz. She is my mother, and moms are the best. They can somehow see in their kids things those same kids can't see in themselves. I don't think my mom has ever heard me preach without crying and saying afterward, "That was the best sermon I have ever heard. I knew you had this in you." Everyone else who says that is generally lying. Cathy Lentz, though, is for real. My mom is always so encouraging that even in my worst moments, she will find a way to see the good in them. She's the type of mom who bails her son out of jail and says, "Well, yes, you committed a crime, but at least it was a felony. If you're gonna make a mistake, make a big one!"[3]

---

[3] I have been arrested only once, and my mom never knew. Until now. Sorry, Mom! I love you!

But now, at thirty-eight years old, I know where my mom got her faith material from. Not weird "you can do it if you believe enough" stuff. I'm talking about the one that says "Yes, there are natural limitations in this life, but God simply does not care." Step-out-in-faith-and-roll-the-dice-and-see-what-happens type faith. The belief that potential is essentially a prison—not a malicious one but a prison nonetheless. Because if you buy into your potential, what you're capable of? Then this life—which should be a wild ride of wins, losses, tears, and joy—never even begins. If you buy into the mentality that you are confined to your potential in this life, it becomes a prison. A prison of limitation and self-reliance and opinions from others who have no idea what truly might be inside you that isn't easy to see right now. I found it really interesting as I learned to truly study the Bible that Jesus refused to accept the limitations people so readily wanted to put on Him. "That guy is a carpenter from a small town." In fact, He was the biggest change agent and culture shifter to ever walk on this Earth. The prison of potential has an unlocked door that keeps a lot of people stuck in it. I have chosen to walk out of that captivity, and that same option is open to everybody.

All this time when my mom would say, "Carl, dream big. Love people. Start again. You have more in you. I believe in you," she was actually quoting a scripture that has become my lifeline, from Ephesians chapter 3, verse 20. It goes like this: "Now to Him who is able to do immeasurably more than all we ask or imagine, according to His power that is at work within us, to Him be the glory in the church and in Christ Jesus throughout all generations, for ever and ever! Amen."

This book is not intended to help people who are content with their potential. I would not be qualified to speak on that. Because if my life represents anything, it's that God has always, and will always, use broken, unqualified people to make a difference in this world. I don't know if you have found yourself in the proverbial bathroom stall at any point in your life. Perhaps you are there right now, or realize you just might be at some point. Please remind yourself that nobody is interested in your potential. Potential has never changed the world. I don't think the God who created you is interested in your potential. I think the God that I believe in is not on the search for "perfect" people. He's on the search for "available" people.

Maybe it's time you start surprising people with what they *didn't* expect from you. A new dream, a new outlook, a new spirit. I think it's time. I want my life to be a giant surprise party when it's all said and done. Maybe one day, people can say about you and me: "Those people surprised me. I didn't think they had it in them."

And we can smile and say, "Oh, we didn't. God did this. And He can do it for you as well."

own the chapter

Often, what we *say* can become what we *see* in our lives. Build a habit of speaking what is right, what is positive, what is healthy even in the face of extreme opposition or negativity. It's more than a positive confession—it's an anchor for your life that won't allow what happens *to* you to change what comes *through* you.

Chapter Two

That's Just the Way It Is

I LIKE BEING ABLE TO control settings when possible. For instance, it can take me at least five tries to get the light settings correct in my own home before I can sit down comfortably. My wife says I'm weird and OCD. I say that I enjoy the pleasure of maximizing the light dimmer I paid for.

"Default" has never been my thing. I don't think it should be anybody's thing, to be clear. Because almost always the default of anything is the most basic, the most average, the most nonspectacular setting. The default of humanity? We have history books full of death, carnage, and self-centered bias. The default of relationships? Two human beings going in opposite directions. If we don't constantly make an effort to break away from the defaults in our own lives—the way we think, the way we love, the way we treat other people—it is a one-way ticket to a life that impacts no one. People who don't know that we actually have an option for more are the people you hear saying things like:

"I was born like this. It's who I am."

"I'm Irish. I drink. It's a national pastime."

"Nobody in my family has ever graduated from college. That's the way it is with us."

"My parents were divorced. Their parents were divorced. I don't want to be divorced, but let's be honest: It runs in the family."

"I'm white. I simply cannot jump, and a dunk contest is not in my future."

Although the last one is actually true,[1] it's a lie that we can't change even the most long-standing types of strongholds in our lives. If you don't like where you sit today, there was a setting that led you there. Every single time. If your life is filled with broken relationships? There is a setting, somewhere in your soul, you have yet to shift. Somewhere you picked up a word, a thought that wasn't true, but you allowed it to drive you to exactly where you are.

Sometimes it helps to look at where you used to be and

---

[1]Shout-out to Brent Barry, though.

where you want to go, to make sure your coordinates look very different. How on Earth people expect to go to new places, achieve new things while making zero new decisions will forever remain a mystery. But not to me. Our default never really dies. We will be drawn to it forever. But we can, without a doubt, make sure we at least know that there are other choices we can make.

Be careful you don't just accept where you are headed because that's the only place you have ever known.

———————

We recently moved our family into a different house. It's only about two miles away from the old one, but we needed more room, our lease was up, and we found a place close by that was great because we didn't have to change our kids' school.

I noticed a funny thing happening the first two weeks after we moved, though. At least five times, I found myself running errands in the car, thinking out loud as I drove home—as I often do—only to look up and realize I was at our old house. I hadn't quite locked in that we had moved, so if I didn't think about it intentionally, that's just where I would drive. I looked at my phone and, sure enough, I never changed my settings to "home." I had a new residence. I just forgot to remind myself. It's funny, and it's happened far too many times.

But you know what I didn't do? I didn't pull up to my old

house, which has new tenants, and just say, "Oh well, here I am. It's not where I want to be, but it's familiar. I'm gonna just go inside, eat some food, and kick it on the couch for a bit. Might as well." No, that's actually a felony called breaking and entering.

This, my friends, is a fantastic picture of what so many people do all the time. "Oh well, this is how I have always thought. This is how I have always been. This is how people have always treated me. That's just the way it is." I beg, with all my heart, to differ. Yes, it will take a while to rechart your life course, and there will be moments where you "sit in an old driveway" that may frustrate you. But reset nonetheless. It's never too late to make a move. It's never too late to start treating people different.

The catch is that nobody else can change your settings but you. You can change your location. You can change your spouse. You can change your occupation. But the old saying rings true: "Wherever you go, there you are." If you think it's already too late? Oh please, think again.

A man in prison reminded me of this through a heartfelt letter that impacted me deeply.

Our church has a TV program that is broadcast all over the world, including into various prisons throughout the United

States. This is particularly important and special to me, because one of my "intentional settings" I am passionate about is that I will never give up on anybody. Everybody is worth honor and dignity in this life, regardless of what they may have done.

I learned this early on, because literally my earliest childhood memory with my dad is not one that takes me back to a baseball game or a birthday party. It takes me back to a prison in Virginia. My dad used to go into jails and preach to the men inside. He would take his Bible and his guitar—truly an epic one-man show. And he would passionately love and encourage these men. And sometimes he would take me with him. I don't remember a lot about specific childhood memories, and I wanted to be sure of recording things accurately. So I called Cathy Lentz, who remembers more random details than the IRS. This was our phone call about those early days watching my parents do what they do.

> *Mom:* Hello?
>
> *Carl:* Mama, thanks for answering the phone. First ring.
>
> *Mom:* I know. It's a miracle, isn't it?
>
> *Carl:* What are you doing?
>
> *Mom:* I just got back from taking the dog to the vet for some blood work. What's happening?

Carl: I'm writing down some stories for my book. One of the stories I want to tell is going with Dad to prisons. How old was I the first time?

Mom: That's when you went to the juvenile detention home in Virginia Beach with Dad. And the whole family, actually, that time. You were only seven when you sat at the table with an eighteen-year-old man who had raped an eighty-year-old woman. You didn't know that. And you were conversing with him. His name was John. I remember that his name was John, and we had refreshments afterward. So that was the first time, at the age of seven, that you sat down at the table—this guy was all by himself. And I don't know what you said to him. I have no memory of that. But I remember on the way back we must've taken two cars. And it was dark, and it was just the car lights inside the car glowing, and I said, "Carl, that was so nice of you to talk to that man." I said, "What was his name?" And you said, "His name was John." And you got tears in your eyes. And then I had trouble driving, thinking, *My gosh, this little guy doesn't even know who that guy was.* I probably went on to say, "You know, he'd done something very bad and he needed to know

Jesus loved him." Or something random—you know what parents say. But it was very touching, actually. Then we left in March of 1986 and moved to Chicago. And then you were taken to Cabrini-Green, and then there was another place called Humboldt—

Carl: Humboldt Park. I remember both those. I remember gunshots. I remember going into that homeless kitchen and Dad rushing us in 'cause there was gunfire.

Mom: Yes, it was just you and him, and you'd gone down in a church van. That's all I remember. I wasn't along on that trip. But when he came back and said you had to wait for bullets to stop shooting, I think I might have said—I'm not sure, but I might've said—"Maybe don't take him down there anymore."

So you can see why I grew up thinking that everybody loves people, and I saw them with grace and compassion. That, yes, those in prison had made mistakes, but that doesn't mean they themselves are a mistake or that the verdict is out on their soul.

Only when I became an adult did I find out that the default setting of our culture is the opposite of believing the best and leaning toward redemption. Most people set out believing the worst and piling on the condemnation. I do remember my dad holding my hand one time as we left a prison, and he said, "Son, don't forget. Every person matters. What a privilege to serve these amazing men."

So, back to our TV show getting into prisons . . . Every week I receive dozens and dozens of letters from people who have been incarcerated. Stories of how they are encouraged, prayer requests because depression is gripping their souls, artwork that is truly spectacular even if all they had was a single pencil. Every week I look forward to reading these letters. But one I will keep with me forever. A man wrote this (edited for more sensitive readers):

Pastor Carl,

Thank you for the work your church does. I watch the show every week, and it's helping me get through this difficult time in prison. I am on year seventeen of a double-life sentence for murder. Most of my life I have spent hating people, blaming people, and have been happy to be set in my ways. Even though I know they led me here. But I watched a sermon you gave the other day, and you talked specifically about racism. How it is

*a sinful, hurtful mind-set that can be changed if we allow God
to open up our minds. During my time in prison, my hatred
for people had increased, especially black people. Prison has
two colors, black or white. After listening to what you said, and
reading the Bible for myself, I'm proud to tell you that I am not
the man I used to be. In fact, I now have many black friends in
this prison that I call "brother." I'm not where I want to be yet
in the way I think. But I'm not where I used to be, as you like
to say. I'm getting better, day by day.*

I cried when I read it. Still do, thinking about it. Because
here is a man who, for all intents and purposes, is "done."
"Forgotten." After all, that is the default prison mind-set, isn't
it? But not for him. He has changed his settings. Perhaps it's
too late in many areas to see the fruit of this reset in his life
outside prison walls. But I know for a fact this man will live a
stronger, more fulfilled life than many will. And all he did was
refuse a default setting he had known his entire life.

———————

If you look at what you believe, what you accept, what you
generate in your life, are there some settings you have not realized are not set in stone? I propose that they are set in pencil.
This moment of this book can serve as an eraser.

Think about somebody who tells you, "That's just the way

it is." It's very possible that my friend in prison is actually far more "free" than that person, who's outside prison walls but is locked up by the self-inflicted settings that have caused them to believe things are unchangeable.

The way it is is the way you set it. Make sure you set it correctly. The way it is is the way you choose it to be. Make sure you have chosen wisely.

I have never been the biggest morning person in the world, and perhaps it had something to do with the sound I heard first waking up. I always set my alarm on my phone, and I honestly didn't realize that you could pick what kind of sound goes with your alarm. Apparently my default alarm was "sound of death and loud noises." I just thought we all had to wake up to that. Until one day my wife, Laura, set her alarm for both of us. I woke up slowly to what sounded like harps, angels' wings fluttering about, and slow ocean waves crashing on a shore. I thought *Am I dreaming? Am I on vacation?* Laura said to me, "You know you have that setting on your phone too, right?" In fact, I did not. Here I am, waking up to a noise I thought everybody was waking up to. It took somebody else to show me that perhaps I have a better option.

We have to fight that temptation to settle for the way it is. Maybe you can wake up to a different mentality tomorrow, and the first step is to realize that yes, you do have some options should you take a look at your settings. What you find, what you see, what you hear might surprise you.

own the chapter

Learning how to "accept and reject" correctly can save our lives. Just because someone has sent something your way—whether in the form of a harsh word, a bad diagnosis, or even the state of your current situation—does not mean you have to accept it. If you have accepted a lower standard in any area of your life, begin to remind yourself that you are worth more, so you can demand more.

Chapter Three

Rearview Mirror

WE MAY BE FROM DIFFERENT places, different races, and different backgrounds, but we all have one thing in common: We have all made mistakes that we regret and would choose to do over if we had another shot. If you have made only good decisions in your life, I will need to see you immediately sprout the wings of an angel, because you are that special!

But for the rest of us, we all have stories, we all have a past, and the difference between people who are effective and people who are not is this: Will you use your story, or will your story use you? When you reflect on your life, what do you remember most? Do you look back and think about all the misses and all the mistakes and all the stuff you didn't do? The time you didn't spend with your kids, the marriage that didn't last, the business that didn't go well? There are people like this all over the world that I have personally met, so I can't even imagine how many deal with this issue.

It's true that there oftentimes isn't anything we can do about our past, but it's equally true that we don't have to be victimized by it either. Being victimized by your past is when you think more about who you used to be and what you used to do more than who you are right now and who you can become tomorrow. The abuse you suffered still haunts you. The bad relationships you suffered through tend to color your potential future ones with a certain negative light. The failure of a previous endeavor gets more time in your thought life than the huge opportunities that lie ahead should you gather enough courage to step out again. Where our past is our main attraction, the key narrative in our story, I actually believe that, if used correctly, it can be a catalyst in our story, one that creates bridges into new territory that we couldn't have reached in any other way.

I love the phrase "If you can't change it, you might as well use it." It is an absolute decision to take control of where you have been, to truly maximize where you can go in this life. But how *you* see *you*—your past, your struggles, your potential— matters more than how anybody else sees you.

I find it amazing how two people can look at the exact

same situation and see polar opposite things. I once saw an afternoon talk show about a condition called body dysmorphia, where essentially an individual looks in the mirror and literally cannot see reality. One of the guests was an extremely beautiful woman who happened to be a model and would in many respects be exactly what our society holds up as "beautiful." The host brought in a full-length mirror and asked her, "What do you see?" Her response was, "I'm fat. My hair is stringy and I see so much gray. My face is hideous." You could hear audible gasps from the audience because it was very plain to see what was happening here: She didn't look anything like the woman she saw in that reflection.

Now, it's easy to judge somebody who has put themselves out there on a show like that and almost feel sorry for them. But the truth is that we all probably struggle with what I call "spiritual past dysmorphia" far more than we would care to admit—where we see all we lack, highlight all the things that have happened in our past that we hate, and we simply dwell on things that in truth have no hold over us but that we can't shake. This spiritual past dysmorphia owns us. Often our reflection isn't our protection—it's our prison. I've often counseled people who suffer from something else I like to call "spiritual selective amnesia"—where it seems as though they only remember the bad things, the failures or the abuses that they have endured. I have to remind them to look a little harder and see that although there is some pain—often real and extreme pain and heartbreak—it has not been *all* bad.

This even works in reverse as well, when people sometimes long for and almost wistfully look back at "the good old days" of their past: "I remember when life was easy. When I didn't have all this family drama. When I could just go out and drink with the boys and didn't have all these responsibilities." And I reply with, "Yes, perhaps, but please remember *it all*. Remember *why* you had so much time: You were broke and had no job. Remember the nights you went out and partied, but please also remember the disease you picked up after that one great night and the paternity suit after that other night and the hours and hours you spent online trying to find people to hang out with." If you are gonna remember the past, let's remember it all.

Our perspective on our past holds so much power that we need to take control over it, make sure we own it. And that it does not, in fact, own us.

———

My whole life story basically comes down to me looking at moments in which I have failed and choosing to use them as fuel for where I want to go. The fact that I am a preacher and a pastor[1] is evidence of this actually working in my life. Because if failure and past mistakes were in charge of job applications, I would be unemployed and considered unfit for duty for almost any calling, *especially* as a preacher.

I struggled with my faith late in my teenage years, and upon entering college I had almost abandoned it completely. I knew I had a passion to help people. I knew I seemed to care about things that others didn't, but there were aspects of my faith that I could not reconcile with the reality of the life I was living and seeing. As a result, I missed so many opportunities to help people and share what I now believe is the most important message in life: God is real, He has a plan, and everybody deserves a chance to hear about it.

The year before I started playing basketball at NC State University, I went to a prep school to improve a few grades and get more exposure as a recruit. I ended up being on one of the best teams in the country, with most of my teammates going on to play big-time Division I basketball and one going straight to the NBA. It was awesome, but also heartbreaking in some ways when I look back at that year.

I was in the racial minority on this team, and the name

---

[1] A pastor *asks* you to do something. A preacher *tells* you to do something, while yelling.

of the game in a situation when you're on a team you really shouldn't be on is to lay low, mind your business, and get through it before anybody finds out you are in way over your head. The problem is that you spend so much time together on a team. Who you are is gonna come out, and there is so much time to talk and opine about all sorts of subjects. Sometimes the conversation would steer from music[2] toward religion, and I would typically excuse myself quietly because I realized no matter what I said or thought, it would not match what others saw or heard in me, and I didn't want to get exposed like that. To make matters worse, a few of my teammates were very charismatic, flamboyant personalities. One in particular was very open about the fact he was a "new school Black Panther" and that he unequivocally hated all white people. One day he said, "Carl, I hate white people. But you cool, though." This was high praise, and in no way did I want to jeopardize my cool white guy status.

One late night, I walked into a conversation revolving around whether Jesus was black, white, or even real. As I sat down in a cold dorm room somebody said, "Carl, don't you know stuff about Jesus? I saw a Bible in your room, and I

---

[2] I remember calling my best friend and hip-hop sage Charles Park to ask about Master P, why his music made me want to join the army and whether or not he did, in fact, have a tank.

heard you pray one time." My response—which is still painful for me to talk or think about—was, "It's not my Bible. I wasn't praying. You have me mixed up. I stay out of all that." And I left.

A few nights later, same topic, same bad timing. I walked in and was asked for a second time, "Yo, please tell this guy that the Bible isn't real. That at best it's a book of ideas, but you can't build a life on it." Now, I knew then and know now I passionately don't believe that. I believe the opposite. Then and now. Yet I declined again, and I would continue to do so whenever I was asked about Jesus or religion the rest of that year.

I would go on to play basketball at NC State, and I mostly lost touch with those guys. But as my life began to change, as one thing led to another and I began to preach and pastor people as my job, I started to go back and try to track down each person I could from that year. Sadly and painfully, I found out that some of my teammates had ended up making bad decisions. One spent time in prison for various things. One got kicked out of an amazing opportunity in the pros due to an inability to control his own behavior. And the list goes on.

There would be times when I would think back on those days of denying my faith, literally walking away from lives that matter, and it would be hard to get out of that dark place of remembrance. I then realized that I can either look back at that time and let it remind me I have no business preaching, no business exhorting others to live passionately and not miss moments in life, because I am as guilty as anybody for failing so many times. Or I can preach like I am a man on fire each and every time, and I can value and think deeply on each interaction I have with somebody because I don't know what tomorrow holds.

One thing I can't do? Forget. So if I'm gonna remember it, I have to choose to see it all—not just the angle that makes me feel like I'm unworthy. I think if you look at your life, how you got to where you are, especially those moments of failure and regret, you can find moments that make you put your head down in shame or discouragement. Those moments are permanent. But the power they have over your life does not have to be. Pick one, begin to see how you can use it instead of how it continues to use you, and slowly but surely your narrative can change. Own your past. Don't let it own you.

———————

Somewhere this week I will most likely find myself onstage preaching to a lot of people. And when I do, you'd better believe I'm going to reflect on my past. But I will not see what disqualifies me. I won't think about the opportunities that I missed, and cut the story short. Because the truth is, my life did not end with those failures. My opportunities to come did not stop because of opportunities wasted. When I do talk about my failures, it will only be to use them as encouragement to remind others what is possible for them. Because I'm still standing. What used to be wounds in my life are now weapons.

Will you allow your reflection to be your protection? There are times when we all have to work hard to remember the good things and the positive moments in a season where it feels like there are not a lot of great things to see. It's the first thing I do as a pastor and friend when I'm talking to somebody who is fighting discouragement and may be overwhelmed with what they feel they have to do to move forward: Rather than go straight to what is not working, I focus on what *is* working. What you *do* love. What is making you smile *right now*. It doesn't negate or minimize the issue at hand, it just changes the position we attack it from.

There was a week where I was personally facing a lot of challenges leading our church in Manhattan. Nothing major, but sometimes a few minor issues that seem to pile up become major in our minds. We needed to find a venue in twenty-four hours because there had been a complication with the one we planned on using for church. We had run out of space to hold our midweek meetings as well, and we didn't have an answer for that challenge either. I had to make a leadership change that week that would affect multiple people and multiple areas, and I knew it would be complex to walk through it all. I needed to get all the way across town to visit somebody who was sick and in the hospital. Each challenge alone, not a problem. But when you add them all up and don't see them with hope and passion, they become problems quickly, internally.

I happened to be in a car with a friend who was from out of town, and he asked me a question that unwittingly helped me that day immensely. He said, "As you reflect on your time here, pastoring this church in this city, what do you think about it? What stands out to you?"

We happened to be crossing a street that I recognized, and I said, "Well, as a matter of fact, I met a guy on that curb there who was so high he couldn't get his balance and was stumbling, to the point that he just had to sit down. We talked for an hour, he ended up coming to church, and now he's a part of our team."

As we kept driving, we passed the Gansevoort Hotel. I said to my friend, "See that right there? There is a club on the top floor, outside. It has a pool. One time we rented the pool, but not the club, to do baptisms. We baptized hundreds of people while all these people in the club watched, and some were so moved they asked to get baptized."

We drove on.

"Right there, in that giant park?" I said. "We had church there once because we couldn't find a venue to rent out. It was probably the coolest service ever, outdoors, packed with people standing. We realized yet again, God will always make a way."

I must have spent the next hour giving my friend way too much detail for a really simple question. And you know what else happened? All those other decisions that I had yet to make and needed to make didn't seem so bad. Didn't seem so impossible. My reflection was my protection that day.

It's your right to exercise this same principle in your life. But like all rights, it means nothing unless exercised. Perhaps it's time to go back and reflect on some mistakes and some failures. And where there may have been definitive periods at the end of some stories. Add a new sentence immediately following the worst moment you can think of. Start it with: "I got up again. I chose to move on." Own it. Walk to the next chapter of your own story.

There is a reason that the rearview mirror in your car is much smaller than your windshield. It's there so you can glance at what is behind you while you stay focused on where you are currently headed. Staring in that rearview mirror for too long can be deadly. The road that lies in the wake of your life thus far is littered with lessons. But they are not leashes. Feel free to own the road that has yet to be paved in your life.

own the chapter

What is normally the outcome when you "take a trip down memory lane"? Does it build your life? Does it put faith in your spirit? If it does not, you need to change what you reflect on. Don't focus on what has not happened in your life. Focus on what still can happen. True leaders don't live in the past. They may glance at it to learn from it, but the future is too important to waste a moment thinking about what can't be changed.

Chapter Four

Fear

FEAR IS BIG BUSINESS IN our world. You can sell products based off fear. You can win elections with a platform rooted in fear. You can motivate people with that one word as your only tagline. You can get rebellious children to actually do something you tell them to do just by evoking the thought of what might happen. You can turn on your TV tonight and learn something new to be scared of that you were never aware of. I saw a TV show the other day with dramatic music and the title "10 Ways People Die in Their Kitchens." You thought your ceiling fan was safe? THINK AGAIN. I had never feared that before. What a great addition.

Fear of what is and fear of what might be: Right there is where fear lives and breathes. It's where fear makes its money—not so much in the reality but in the hypothetical. I tell people all the time that there are enough real things in this life to fear that we don't need to compound the issue by making up even more things to *potentially* be afraid of.

———

I wonder how you handle fear: fear of the known, and fear of the unknown. In regard to the former, this is difficult for us all to manage. I'm not a big acronym fan to begin with, but one in particular has always bugged me. People say, "Fear is not real. It stands for *False Evidence Appearing Real.*" Sounds great. Only problem is *it's* patently false. Sometimes we have good reason to fear. Recognizing things isn't the problem. I don't fear swimming with sharks because I make up how nasty they are. I fear sharks because sharks eat people all the time. This is not false evidence. This is called "Shark Week" on TV. So I'm not the guy telling you to look fear "dead in the face" and say, "It's not real." I am the guy who is a believer that fear is a part of all of our lives. Those who learn how to deal with it end up making an impact in this world. If I look at the path my life has taken thus far, every single "door of opportunity" would have had a giant neon blinking sign above it that read "FEAR."

I was nineteen when I decided to leave NC State and go study the Bible. I played basketball my whole life, somehow got lucky enough to land a spot on an ACC basketball team[1], and loved every second of it. I still hold the ACC record for most warm-up three-pointers made, and it's not even close.

I found a niche on our team quickly as I realized basically from day one that my athletic ability was not going to be what kept me on the team. I was good, and I'm still good. But when you play on that level, you find out quickly that there are levels of good.

I remember meeting my now best friend, Adam Harrington, first day on campus. He was a highly touted recruit, coming out of a high school in Massachusetts where he scored over 47 million career points or something. We walked to the gym together that first day, and I said, "You want to play one-on-one?" He was like, "Sure." Our game lasted about three minutes, as I found out immediately that Adam was born the wrong color. Although he appeared to be white, his forty-two-inch vertical and insane basketball IQ led me to believe he was in fact black. I was so overmatched I said, "Bro, you just shoot and I'll rebound."

But I found my way on that team and planned on being

---

[1] People are still trying to figure out how the system failed and I made it.

there for a long time. My coaching staff at the time was filled with the now *Who's Who* of college basketball coaching. My head coach was Herb Sendek, who to this day is one of the best, smartest, and greatest coaches I have ever known. His lead assistant was Sean Miller: the same Sean Miller who is now perhaps the best coach in the game.[2] And the director of basketball operations was Mark Phelps, who went on to be a head coach and currently helps Miller lead Arizona as his assistant. I will always be grateful to Mark, who went above and beyond to help me play college basketball. I had a plan mapped out that I was absolutely certain was going to work. I would play all four years, get right into coaching, and make millions and millions of dollars, telling athletes much better than I to do things.

Then one hot summer July day on a quick visit home to Virginia Beach to see my parents, I walked into a church. A pastor named Steve Kelly was preaching, and I don't know what happened exactly but he said something along the lines of "There is somebody in here that needs to make a change. You have known religion, but you have never known who Jesus is. You are afraid to surrender all, and I have bad news for you. If Jesus Christ is not Lord of all, He is not Lord *at all*."

[2]And who I think should coach the New York Knicks right now.

Now, I have a real palpable disdain for religious jargon. I grew up in church. I ran from church. I know a real Christian from a churchgoing nominal Christian better than most. And this was different. He may have been talking to somebody else in that room, but Steve Kelly was absolutely talking to me. In many ways my life was great. Most people always assume that you have to have some rock-bottom story to find God. They are wrong. God is so good He will find you on your little mountaintop too, if you let Him.

That day I reluctantly put my hand up and asked him to pray with me. I was scared. I was riddled with fear. Things like "What if this isn't real?" "What if this means I have to give up everything that I love?" "What if this means that for the rest of my life I have to listen to terrible Christian music and wear pleated khaki pants and get a haircut that looks like literally every single Alabama football fan?" These were real fears. But I walked through that fear, because what that door offered was too good to pass up.

And let me be really clear: I believe Jesus is real. I follow Him, and I believe in Him. You don't have to. And if you scoff at my belief, please know I'm scoffing right back at you times ten, because you believe something outlandish as well. Let's just all agree that what we believe is going to take faith. But choosing to "follow Jesus" does not mean the end of fear. Not at all. In fact, it's almost like you welcome more fear. You quickly find out, as a Christian, that when Jesus said, "Come and follow Me," He conveniently left out "and oftentimes you will do so crying, yelling, and looking like a kid being pulled by the arm through an amusement park the kid doesn't want to leave." Being a Christian means the end of the reign of fear and sin in your life. Both are still there. But they do not own you. We believe God's grace meets you where you are at and will not leave you like that. You can't "make yourself better" or "work your way to God." These are lies. We are all sinners, we all have issues, and what Jesus claims is that only He can save us and that only He can sustain us. You don't have to believe this at all, but it has to be said to put in context why I think fear can be fantastic fuel in our lives rather than fatigue-inducing quicksand that holds us back.

So I left church that day and began to actually apply what I was hearing. I thought, *You know what? I'm going to search this out for myself.* And I made the fearful decision to head to Sydney, Australia, to study the Bible. Fear was literally my launching pad. I was walking away from a surefire plan. I was traveling to another planet—which Australia basically is—to try some things I had never tried. My calling, my wife, Laura, my church, my passion—all were behind the scariest door of all time.

Since that day, this remains exactly true: Fear never leaves. But the way we handle it can always change.

If you are reading this and I have begun to even remotely convince you that fear is real but what's *behind* the fear is better, I will say this: It all starts with a step. Fear is paralyzing by nature. So many people never get over fear because they are waiting for a feeling to combat the fear. If this "feeling" exists, please, somebody, send me its email so I can ask where the hell it's been my whole life. The only way you get through any fear is to step up, even minimally. And if you survive, it means it wasn't as bad as you thought. And slowly but surely fear loses its grip.

Over the years, I have had the honor to speak and preach to a lot of people. Sometimes, huge crowds. After years and years of doing this, yes, it does get easier. But I vividly remember the small, constant steps I took to walk directly into fear and keep going. I remember preaching my heart out one time at a meeting mostly filled with young people. There may have been 150 people listening. I was growing in my confidence, but speaking to young people is perhaps more difficult than any other group because attention spans are low. Some had no say in whether they actually wanted to be listening to you in the first place. And although young people might not say anything, they have this unique ability to suck the confidence right out of you with that look on their face that seems to scream, "You are boring me, I don't like you, and I can't wait until you stop talking."[3]

After I was done, an adult who happened to be in the room said, "Hey, great job up there. But y'all are going to have to get new carpet, because I think you burned a hole in it with all that pacing that you did." When I went back to watch the recording, I didn't realize that I must have channeled all my fear into my feet. No wonder these kids couldn't pay attention. It was like I was an Olympic speed walker up there going back and forth on the stage. But I did it. And I didn't let that embarrassing rewind stop me from walking forward.

That day was a step. The next time was a step. Fear doesn't normally get knocked out in the first round of the fight. More often, you win your fight in a split decision judges call after a twelve-round battle that looked like it was in doubt the whole time. The key is just to keep fighting, keep swinging, and never stop.

If you fear trusting somebody because you have been burned so many times, you don't need to go on a date. You need to sit down in a quiet moment and remind yourself, *There are still good people in this world, and I will find them.* It's a step. If

[3]By the way, huge love and respect to all the youth pastors out there reading this. What you see is not what you get with these young people, who preach and serve so faithfully. The most annoying ones end up being the best leaders! So preach on.

you fear large crowds, you don't need to go to the Thanksgiving Day parade in NYC. You need to take a walk with a friend, and the next week ask another friend. Step by step, we win in this life.

There will come a day—if you're Christian, God will do this; if you are not, hopefully a good friend will try to do this—where you need to skip some steps and jump right into something. Have you ever seen somebody inch their way into a pool to test the temperature only to see a friend come up beside them and shove them in? That needs to happen sometimes as well. But taking small steps puts you in a position to realize: *I actually have more control over this than I think I do.* I don't know what step you need to take, but it needs to happen now.

———————

Fear is a fantastic fuel, but it is a terrible boss. My relationship with fear-defiance—not fear-avoidance (massive difference)— began back around the same time I left college. I went out to L.A. to save money and figure out some things before Australia. I got a job working at Gucci, on Rodeo Drive. I was the guy who stands at the door and opens it. Seriously, that was my job. It was a step in the right direction, but it also opened up new fears, which you find out happens frequently. I still feared getting to know people, and I definitely feared sharing my new faith.

I remember one time saying to God, "I will do whatever You ask. But I definitely won't be a preacher. I don't know enough and I'm too shy." That's funny to say now, and sometimes people don't believe me, but that is the truth. So here I am, a guy who is, yes, a committed Christian, but still facing down fears that truly worried me. How would I get money for Australia? At the doorman rate, I'd have enough by 2034. How would I ever be effective as a Christian if I couldn't muster up the courage to even tell a random stranger what I believe?

I remember calling my dad, who is still the GMA,[4] and sharing these concerns. And he said, "Son, just change a little each day. Save your money. Tomorrow have one less coffee. Tomorrow find a way to say hi to somebody. Don't worry about preaching all you know.[5] Just win the fight against fear by starting a conversation."

So that became my goal. The next day, that was my big mission: "I'm going to tell a random stranger that they are awesome, and that God can use them." I realize this was not an Earth-shattering thing to say, but before I became a Christian I didn't even *acknowledge* people I didn't know, let alone prepackage a greeting. But it was something.

[4]Greatest Man Alive.
[5]That would have taken an entire three seconds.

A man came rolling around the corner and into Gucci. And if you are familiar with this scene, often people walk around like they actually own the air you breathe. It's amazing and funny. But this guy was probably sixty, and he looked like a cross between the magician Criss Angel, a rapper who wears all his chains on the same day, and Danny DeVito. Mix those together and you can see this guy. The woman he had with him looked exactly like you think she would. You could safely surmise that, due to the age gap, she was with him for his great personality.

When he walked in, I thought, *That's the guy. When he walks out, I'm going to get him.* Thirty minutes later he walks out, and I open the door. Keep in mind we were under strict instructions to not speak, ever, as doormen. Just open the door and close the door. And I said, "Have a nice day. You're amazing, and God is going to use you to do great things."

We have all had moments where you say things, and you can almost see the words you said floating out of your mouth, and you try but cannot grab them as they slip through your cold, soon-to-be-dead fingers. That's how I felt right then.

He looked at me and said, "What did you say to me?"

I said, "Sir, I'm sorry. I said you're awesome, and God is going to use you to do great things."

He said, "You don't even know me! Why would you even speak to me!"

I apologized and asked God to remove me from Earth. And the guy walked away in a hurry.

I spent the next few moments questioning life. Every fear is compounded in moments where you think failure rules the day. Remember that. Let each failure stand or fall on its own. They are not always linked. When someone tells you, "Bad things happen in threes," tell them, "Only if you mean getting advice from you two more times."

To my surprise, that man came rolling back around that same corner an hour later. He was making a beeline for me. And I thought, *Yep. This is the way I go out. Killed by a rich guy at the door of Gucci. And I never actually bought anything from Gucci.*

But what he said I will never forget.

He said, "Tell me what you said again."

I did.

He said, "So you are just a door guy that says nice things to people?"

I said, "Well, when you put it like that, I guess I am."

He said, "What do you believe gives you the confidence to tell me something like that?"

And right then I forgot about my fear. I forgot about what I did not know and spoke only about what I did know. I told him about what happened to me. About what I now believe about Jesus. About how He—not a church, not a method, not a religion—can change anybody. God is not on the lookout for perfect people. There are none. He's on the lookout for *available* people. And I am one.

He said, "When you clock out today, come by my office. I want to talk to you."

When I saw the address on his business card and the floor number of the building, I thought he was either a big-time CEO or that I would be pushed from that rooftop. But I reluctantly went.

The office looked like a Versace corporate office. I think the soap in the bathroom had diamonds embedded in it. I sat down in front of his sprawling desk. And he looked at me and said, "I don't know if I believe what you said. I am not a good man. But what you said has stuck with me. I don't know what you will end up doing someday, but I hope it has to do with speaking to people. Here is a check for $2,500. I hope it helps you on your journey."

I took the check, shook his hand, and said something amazing, like, "Thanks. Catch you around town. It's been good." And I ran out of there in case he changed his mind.

This man did not know me, did not know that my savings goal was two thousand dollars to be able to make the move to Australia happen. And I did not know that my decision to face one fear would equate to roughly three other fears—and that it would aid and abet my plan to walk into my next chapter.

I'm not sure what you fear today—whether it's real or whether it's imagined or whether your next step hypothetically keeps you up at night because it's so riddled with fear. But I know this: Life is too short for you to live enslaved by fear. I would rather die proving a fear right than live never testing the waters because fear talked me into staying in a boat that was actually floating in two feet of water. No way.

Pick one thing you are absolutely afraid of today. Write it down. And then above it, write: *I WILL OVERCOME THIS*. You never know what random blessing is going to come around a corner in your life with a breakthrough in its pocket.

I still have fear in my life. Fear of what might be, sometimes of what is. But one fear I will never allow to take residence in my life is the fear of "What if I didn't try?" Not me. I want to tell my grandkids someday, "I was the worst thing that ever happened to fear. I put it out of business."

One thing is for sure: You are doing better than you think you are, and fear has a time limit on it. You control that clock, nobody else. I pray the time is up on fear in your life. If fear has been king, I think its reign of terror is over for you.

own the chapter

Fear is unavoidable. We can either face it head-on and begin to use it as fuel or we can run from it and allow it to have far more influence on us than it deserves to have. Since fear breeds more fear, primarily in isolation, the best thing we can do to overcome it is "call for backup." The moment we talk about what scares us, it begins to lose its power on our lives. Sometimes all we need is another set of eyes on a situation to remind us that we can get through anything. Those who walk alone, fall alone. But those who surround themselves with strength are always strengthened. Choose a relationship you trust, be vulnerable and open, and be prepared to live a life marked by faith, not fear.

Chapter Five

Gold in the Garbage

BRIAN HOUSTON'S SON JOEL WAS the first person I met when I got to Australia, and we have been best friends since that day. He was the best man at my wedding, I was able to officiate his, and we currently lead our church in NYC together. If you don't know Joel, a quick summary: He is a world-renowned songwriter for Hillsong Church and Hillsong United,[1] and has carved a new path for "worship" music that has impacted countless people. That is what he is known for "doing." *Who* he is, however, is even better. I remember

---

[1]Also known as the greatest band to not win a Grammy, because the Grammy people are silly.

loving the songs Joel wrote, and then, after meeting him and spending more time with him, thinking, *When is this guy going to realize I'm not really that good at anything?* Apparently, that has yet to happen, because Joel is busy. Good for me. Because I'm still surprised I get to be in his life at all.

Just as he has this ability to find a melody in a song others would overlook, he always manages to find the good in a person that others would not even want to find. In both cases he can take something that could be discarded and find some diamonds in it.

One night after we left Hillsong Conference in Sydney, which is a once-a-year gathering of Christians that packs giant arenas all over the world, we drove through Kings Cross. It's a part of Sydney that is now a little more palatable these days, but at the time it was known for its drugs and prostitution, and in general was not the place you'd want to take a nice late-night walk. But we were both hungry and decided to get some pizza. At one street corner there was a very dilapidated house. There were rows and rows of them, in fact, but this one was especially unwelcoming. I'll never forget the flickering blue light that cast a haze over its doorstep. It was creepy and weird, and I thought to myself, *This is probably the wrong street to be on.*

As I went to walk away, Joel said, "Do you hear that?" I told him I didn't hear anything, but before I knew it, Joel had hopped a little fence and was making his way to the porch. I followed, because that's what real friends do. If we are going to make stupid decisions, we make them together.

There were used needles all over the ground and a stench that anybody who has worked on the streets or helped out the homeless in any city would know immediately. And under that flickering blue light was a giant garbage bag. We stared at it for a moment, and both of us noticed that it moved ever so slightly. Honestly, I wanted to run. But Joel walked up to it while I prayed that this would not be the last adventure of my life.

We opened up the bag, and what we saw was not an animal. It was a person. A human being. His eyes opened, and he blinked slowly, as if that blue light was an alarm his eyes hadn't seen for a while. I gasped. Joel and I both fought back tears. I remember saying, "Sir, are you okay? Can we help you?"

I will never forget his sweet, reluctant smile as he said, "Sure. That would be nice. How are you guys?"

His voice sounded like it had not been used in a long time.

The drive home that night after we left our new friend was more quiet than normal. Neither of us mentioned the smell or the needles we were navigating around. It's not every day you find gold in the form of a living, breathing person in the literal garbage of life.

Maybe it should be.

Few people can hear a melody the way Joel Houston

can—or find an unproven young songwriter who turns out to be prolific once given an opportunity. Yet we can all tune our ears, fix our eyes, and set our hearts on the things in this life that can be experienced only when we overlook nothing and take inventory of everything: Our children. Our jobs. Our friendships. Our "daily grind." There is more gold in the garbage, to be sure. Gold in the form of people who have been written off due to bad decisions. Gold in the form of ideas that perhaps one person said couldn't work but if another set of eyes looks at it could be an idea that changes the world.

I don't know the story behind what led to that man finding himself homeless and distraught and finding rest in a trash bag. I don't need to. Because I realized that day, no matter what the circumstances were, he was still a person with a future. With possibilities. But if we don't learn to see the good in people, the hope in the failure, the redemption in some of the wreckage of this life, maybe it won't be as dramatic as finding somebody so discarded that he was literally thrown away. It's possible we can throw away relationships, throw away passion, throw away lessons that we deem to be "garbage" but in fact could be gold in the form of perspective that we can use down the road.

I am a big believer in getting the right people around you, to help you see things that we may miss—about our own lives, about our choices, about blind spots we can't see in general.

It's vital. But I often find myself asking people what *they* see about themselves. Because at the end of the day, that's what will make the difference in this life. Sometimes it's just going to be you who believes in something. Can you believe in something you're passionate about? Can you take a risk and step out even if nobody else can see it? Joel and I walked by the same street, looked at the same porch, but only he saw that bag that moved. If it was up to me, we would have kept moving. I saw garbage. Joel saw something more.

I have found this ability to see something deeper, when I activate it in my own life, to be very, very useful. Sometimes people have written me off, for a million different reasons— questioned what I see, what I believe, who I choose to invest in. But I've worked hard at making sure that if I believe something, if I see potential in something, I don't need a fan club to support me. I don't need further validation or approval. Just because somebody else does not see it? Doesn't mean I have to believe it's not there.

I walked into a prison my first year as a real pastor. I say real, because I had an actual pastoral ID card. I'm not sure it's worth a thing in this life, especially now that you can hop online and basically become a "minister" overnight to officiate a wedding or for whatever it may be you need a minister's license for. But to me? I was excited. I had graduated from Bible college, worked really hard to put myself in the best position

I could to be effective moving forward. So naturally, heading to a prison to see an old friend who made a bad decision was going to be one of my first stops where I could actually use my ministerial credential.

Most prisons have a system where clergy or pastors can come visit at different times than the general public. So I walked up to the check-in desk and told the woman who I came to see, and she promptly cut me off midsentence and told me that regular visit times were over for the week. I explained that I was a pastor.

She looked at me and said, "You ain't no pastor. You don't look like no pastor. Come back during regular visiting hours."

I said, "Ma'am, I am a pastor. Here is my pastoral credential and identification card."

She proceeded to tell me, "That ain't real. You can get that overnight at Kinko's. You ain't getting in here, so you might as well go home."

I thought about my options—there were none—hung my head, and went home. I decided I would go back the next day, only this time I would have my ID card *and* I would take my framed bible college diploma, which was relatively large and heavy, just to really drive home the point.

When I walked up that next day, she saw me coming and said, "You again?"

I said, "Ma'am, I realize you may have a stressful job and

might have made a mistake yesterday. So here is my ID, and I brought my diploma of ministry as well."

She looked at me and said, "Boy, let me tell you something. I go to church. I have a pastor. And he doesn't look like you. You don't even look like a Christian, let alone a pastor. Matter of fact you don't look like much at all! And if you come back again, we are going to have a problem."

I walked out of that jail, stunned, sad, and couldn't help but think of the irony of my crazy life. Here I am, lucky to not be in jail, now being stopped from trying to get in jail. As silly as it was, it rattled me. Some situations are like that. They land at the right time, for the wrong reasons, in your soul, and start to create thoughts that lead to discouragement. This was happening to me. *Maybe I don't look like a pastor. Maybe I should change the way I look or talk or something. If I can't even get into a jail to encourage one person, what hope do I have of doing this anyway?*

After some thought, I woke up with a defiant, resilient spirit and said to myself, "I'm gonna get into that jail." Conforming was not an option. Looking like a regular pastor, whatever that means? Not an option. I was fresh out of khaki pants, a button-up shirt from the Gap, and some brown shoes. Giving up wasn't an option, either.

I remembered that I had one card I had yet to play. My friend was a part of the Norfolk PD SWAT Division. So I called him and told him my dilemma. He laughed and said that although he didn't blame the lady for making a judgment—because the first time he came to my church, he thought the exact same thing—this would not stand. He accompanied me to the prison the next day, and walked me right by the lady at the front window. I absolutely gave her the most patronizing smile and wave I could because I'm a work in progress and this book is called *Own the Moment,* not *I Claim to Be Perfect.*

I got to see my friend through that awful glass that separated us. And as we talked, our conversation landed on one topic. He told me, "Bro, people treat us like we are garbage in here. I'm afraid I'm going to start to believe it."

I told him, "Over my dead body." That it doesn't matter how people treat you, how they label you, as long as *you* don't label you. His life was not over. He would recover. And I was proud to know him. He made a decision to find the "gold" in each day. Might be a ray of sun through his prison-cell sliver of a window. Could be a beautiful conversation in a very ugly surrounding with a new friend he didn't expect to make. That's what life is about sometimes. Finding the good in the middle of a whole lot of bad.

Upon his release, he reminded me that he would still apply the "gold in the garbage" mentality even though he was free. It's really hard to hold somebody back who refuses to stop digging and fighting and searching for hope in a hopeless culture or situation. I have no doubt my friend will keep shining for the rest of his life.

As for the lady at the window? When I left, she said, "I'm sorry I didn't believe you were a pastor."

I told her, "It's okay. Because *I* believe I am."

She ended up coming to our church and loving every second of it.

It's amazing what can happen when we refuse to settle for the garbage view and stay dedicated to the golden one. I don't see New York City as a place full of traffic. I see it as a place where I have so much time to think in the car. I don't see drug dealers as simply people who break the law. I see them as people with potential to lead a really good community group in our church someday because they obviously know how to get a message through the streets. I don't see drug addicts as people who will be lucky to just make it by someday. I see them as people who will have one powerful story of overcoming an issue that had a death grip on them at one point in their lives.

You see garbage? Show me, and I promise you I will find some gold in it. Not because I was born like it or am some holy "man of god." Because I have trained myself to see it. You can, too. Tonight, I will pray for that man Joel and I found so many years ago. I will pray again that I never stop seeing the other side of the coin, the possibility of redemption, the audacious view that hope can arise in the middle of the worst of situations.

This week as you go about your life, make sure you double-check the "trash." Who knows what treasure might lie within it.

own the chapter

We are all guilty of not seeing something for what it's truly worth. Maybe it's time for you to reevaluate some things and take another look. One time, I threw a pair of shorts away as I cleaned out an old closet. I took one last look in this bag of trash before I turned away and sure enough, I saw a $100 bill peeking out of the pocket of those old shorts. Always the best feeling ever. There is, without a doubt, a relationship in your life that has more good in it than you realize. Take inventory, look at your life with "fresh eyes," and see what gold you can find hiding in plain sight.

Chapter Six

To All the Ladies in the Place
with Style and Grace

"I'M NOT READY FOR THAT."

How many times have you heard that? How many times have you *said* that? It's a very natural reaction to things that are daunting and often make us feel insecure. It's also a very common excuse to bow out of things we need to step into. I love being prepared, I love having what I think I need to get something done, and I love a clear plan that eliminates needless effort. But the "myth of ready" is that there will come a point where you have exactly what you need, for the right situation, for that breakthrough down the road, for that moment. What's ironic is that no matter how much planning you do, studying you do, life will knock the wind out of you so quick you end up falling back on who you are in the moments way more than what you "know." A very famous Broadway actor who also used to box named Mike Tyson said, "Everybody has a plan until you get punched in the mouth." I love that because it's so true.

Sometimes you need to get as ready as you can, but realize that none of us are complete. None of us possesses all the things we need to do what we are called to do yet. At some point, you have to step out in life even if your metaphorical "outfit" is not right. How many dates have been stalled or delayed because somebody was furiously getting ready for what seems like hours? At some point you gotta work with what you got.

———

Speaking of dates and relationships in general, there are far too many people who are either in the wrong relationship because of the myth of ready, or not in a relationship at all. Both for the exact same reason. I've seen idealistic people think, "I'm not ready for a serious relationship, so I'll just date and look around, and although this relationship isn't the best or super serious it's cool because I'm not ready for that anyway." This simply leads many into a not-serious serious relationship. There are no placeholder relationships. The one you are in is making you better or worse, as the broken record spins out of control on that statement.

I wouldn't say that Laura and I are relationship experts, but I would say we are very close to being that due to a huge component of our job as pastors helping people make the right connections in life and disconnections in life. I've talked to a lot of men who sit waiting, trying to get better, trying to get their lives in order to be "ready" for that special somebody. To a degree? Fantastic. Please believe that the day some boy tries to date either of my daughters, the list of questions I have is so severe and so long and so threatening I have no doubt that poor guy will walk out the door in shame. As he should—good riddance. Nobody will ever be good enough for my daughters, end of story.

But for everybody else? Who said you were going to be ready for this type of love anyway? To the ladies reading this, you are far from exempt. In fact, I've told some single women Laura and I love that while they are "getting ready" or as some say "being picky," the love boat floats on, with or without you. And here is the worst/best part of it all anyway, depending on how you look at it. You don't really get to know somebody until after real commitment is made. After some time, some battles, some wins and losses. I laugh and smile when a couple has dated, gotten engaged, and close to the wedding they say, "We know each other. It's time." Hilarious. You know what dating is called? A presentation. It's a tryout.

Incidentally, this is exactly why we are huge proponents of people not having sex until they are actually married. Yes, we are Christians and we believe this honors God and is not remotely optional, regardless of how many people try to say otherwise. But it's also common sense. Sex is so vital, so important, such an incredible part of a relationship that it would make sense to keep this in its proper place. A lot of people use sex as a cover for what they feel they lack. Because they are insecure about what they can't offer. Men advocate for sex early, because they know if they can make this link, the connection is "stronger" in their mind. Women often have sex early in a relationship because if they feel insecure about what they offer, sex will prove they can give something that is wanted.

Problem is, sex is not the best offering of a human being. But if this card is played early, 45 million steps of relational building are skipped. What should be intimate is cheap and the relationship begins to malfunction. A guy once told me, "But Pastor Carl, I have to see if we are physically compatible. What if I get married, and then we find out there is no spark in the bedroom? We don't connect?" I told him,

"So somebody told you sexual compatibility comes down to physicality? Who told you this? Sex is almost all about emotional and spiritual fulfillment that drives the physical connection. Love is what fuels great sexual fulfillment. Not 'feeling compatibility.'" For many men, it's obvious there is no Wi-Fi in the cave they still live in. This is the only explanation for the repetitive nature of relationship-ruining by stupidity.

My point in saying all of this is that what we think makes us ready is making us more "unready." We rush important things that can make us better, because of these myths.

I always say you need to date somebody long enough to firstly let a cycle of medication wear off. Go on a date with somebody for an entire day. Secondly, date somebody for the entire calendar of seasons. New York City is very different in July than it is in January. Imagine visiting Manhattan in July, being hot on the subway, walking around in some flip-flops and then saying, "You know what, I'm in. The climate is perfect. I shall buy a house today." Come January? When those absolutely biting winds howl down those Brooklyn streets and seem to slap you in the face with an evil type of cold that *actually* ruins your day? We would have zero sympathy for the person sitting on the curb crying, freezing in flip-flops and saying, "I just can't believe this. This always happens to me.

It was supposed to be warm." This is the person who rushes relational "readiness," lives on false security, and is now involved deeply with a person they should absolutely not be connected to.

So what am I trying to say? Perhaps the people who are "ready" simply seem that way because they have embraced a comfortable peace with a state of "unready." Meaning, they are not waiting to "feel perfect" before they step into something. They are not overlooking amazing people who have flaws and deeming them "unready" either. There is a nuance to the reality of ready that destroys the myth of ready that you can only find when you get off your couch, out of your mirror and go try a dance or two. In relationships and in life.

I was not "ready" to preach. But I worked on who I was. So when I stepped out to do it? I found my "readiness" on the fly. Laura and I were not "ready" to have children. Nobody ever is. But we had them.[1] We love each other. We did the best we can to be the best we could and can be for our kids. The rest we have had to learn. I'm so glad I have these three kids. I couldn't have prepared for them. They are too spectacular. Perhaps fear could have kept me from even trying to be a good dad.

---

[1]And thoroughly enjoyed conceiving them, I must add.

———————

And as I think about it? I was *not* ready to marry one Ms. Laura Jayne Brett. I remember the day a certain man might have saved me from missing out on the woman of my dreams.

I was an intern for Brian Houston, my pastor and my boss, and one of my heroes. We sat down one day for coffee and he said to me, "So, how long do you think you will date Laura before you ask her to marry you?"

I looked at him with a mix of incredulity and sheepishness and said, "Well, it's still early. I'm working on a lot of stuff in my own life, and I know I'm not ready."

Brian said, "Ready? Who told you 'ready' had anything to do with it? Plus, you are right about one thing: You are a mess. But you're under construction. You will be until you die."

Brian Houston and subtlety are not friends, at all.

He continued, "Do you love her?"

I said, "With my whole heart."

He said, "Does she love you?"

I said, "From what I know. But that's the thing. She doesn't know all about some of my weak areas."

He said, "No, you're wrong. She does. We have talked. But she has chosen to love you despite them. If you don't have some courage, you will lose a woman like Laura. She's too secure to waste any time."

When I tell you I left his office like my feet were on fire, I'm understating it. He made so much sense, and I realized how little sense I was making previously. I had a long history of really bad relationships. I was sexually reckless and had the scars in my soul to prove it. Laura was so sharp, so secure that she had dated only two guys before me. *Dated.* So I felt unworthy. As if I could somehow replace my bad times prior with months or years of "good living" to show her I was ready.

I realized that I was simply never going to magically "heal" and that I needed to still lead and still love and still risk while injured. Emotionally ready? I would never be. But I saw a counselor two times a week, and had men I trusted challenging me on areas I didn't want to confront. Maybe being emotionally ready really comes down to being emotionally honest.

I also had two jobs at the time and had very little idea about where I was headed upon my Australian departure after Bible college was over except I knew I wanted to serve in a church. I was working hard to save money, to have something to show her father—and maybe myself—that I was "ready." As if my $2,000 of savings would wow her father. Lord help me. Financially ready? Again, I was coming up empty. But I kept every job I took, and my employers loved me. I stuck to a budget and saved my money and was practicing for the day that maybe I would have money. Being financially ready comes down to what values you have, not how many valuables you possess.

As I went down the list of all the things that were holding me back from asking Laura if she would be my wife, I was ready to stop trying to be ready. And I made the best decision of my life: to marry Laura Brett.

———————

I will never forget asking her father, Kevin Brett, for his daughter's hand in marriage. I said, "Sir, I don't have all I will have. I'm not sure about what life is going to bring our way. But I know this: I will love your daughter till the day I die, and that will never change."

He told me, "Son, that's all I had going for me when I got married. It was enough. You will work the rest out on the way. You two will do great things together."

He looked at my unreadiness but saw *me* in the middle. I'm forever grateful he did. I've been madly in love with his daughter now for a long time.

You know what I find the most fascinating about being married to her, going on fifteen years now? She always changes. She has new passions. She has new desires. She has new grace in her life, all the time. I have to wake up tomorrow and learn about her. Listen to her. Investigate the love of my life. To find out what I need to do to make her feel more loved every day. She was out of my league the first time I saw her, with some faded Lee jeans and flowing black hair and a magnetic, radiant smile that turned my head instantly. She is still out of my league.

I'm so glad I didn't wait to get ready, to climb to her level before I took a chance. To think we will ever be ready for the greatest things in this life is sometimes insulting to the greatness and ever-changing nature of the very essence of this life, which is change itself. You may not be where you want to be right now, but I can almost guarantee that you are not where you used to be.

I propose to you today to live prepared to be unready sometimes. The moment matters too much.

This past year, I took my daughter Ava to her first school dance. More accurately, I drove her and dropped her off and was banned by my daughter from coming any closer than two miles for the rest of the night. I was waiting at the bottom of the stairs as she bounded down with a bright smile and a gorgeous demeanor.

She said, "Dad, you ready?"

I said, "In no way, girl, am I ready to take you to this dance and watch you walk in without me. But let's go. Wouldn't miss it for the world."

Such is life. If it matters enough, be ready to go. Even if the proposition makes you unsteady. The adventure rages on, with or without us.

I know what I'm choosing.

own the chapter

Waiting to be ready can become a robbery. It can steal the joy of a new faith-step and the confidence you can only gain from taking risks and stepping out into the unknown. How many things in life would you have already tried if you didn't fear failure? Additionally, how many people in your life might you be holding to an unrealistic standard of completeness when you too have areas that are in the process of healing? I always have held the view that I want to give people the same grace I want them to give me. It doesn't stop me from having high standards for myself or for others, but it gives me patience as I realize that everybody is on this journey, together. Put this type of grace in action in your life and the product will be better relationships.

Chapter Seven

The Deserted Island Challenge

I BELIEVE THERE ARE MOMENTS hidden within the monotony of life. We all understand the law of diminishing returns, where the more you do something, the more the temptation to not appreciate or maximize that particular thing increases dramatically. The problem here is, What if that "thing" is life itself? What if what should be an encounter-rich, adventure-plenty journey becomes the often-referenced "daily grind"? Another day, another struggle: The "dream job" becomes the "nine to five." The marriage you could not wait for becomes "the ball and chain." The business you used to stay up at night dreaming about and planning for becomes "so much responsibility . . . I wish I could go back to simpler times."

We have all been there. I have had to teach myself to not ask God to deliver me from my own prayer requests. I'm guilty of asking God to "use my life" and then complaining to Him down the road, "Lord, I feel like people are using me." I once prayed that God would "use me like a bridge"—where I could use my life as a connection to God for others who perhaps would not find Him any other way. Not long after, I expressed to my wife that I felt like people were walking all over me at times. Her notoriously quick-witted response: "Babe, that sounds a whole lot like a bridge to me."[1]

I think the beauty in this life comes from the ability to look through the monotony, through the normal, and perhaps extract something meaningful from what otherwise doesn't look that special. How many times have you been surprised to hear somebody's story after you took the time to listen? That's why I refuse to believe that there are "special people" in this world. I think *everybody* has special value. Our problem is that we don't have enough time to find what is too often hidden.

I fly often, and you build habits and rituals as you do this to keep your sanity. Rarely do flights depart on time, rarely do

---

[1] Huge shout-out to wives all over, who shoot down their husband's cry-me-a-river marathons.

things go exactly as planned, so you have to make up little games or odd hypotheticals to keep the time moving. One of my favorites, perhaps morbidly, is to imagine: *If this plane went down over a deserted island, who would I want to make alliances with immediately?* Who would help me rule this island? Obviously, this island would be mine, and I would need people to help me run it.

You quickly eliminate the people with too much carry-on baggage, because that reveals entirely too much about them already. You really needed seventeen bags and expected to fit that grand piano in the overhead space? Immediately eliminated.

You then cross off the loud talkers. People who do this in airports and on planes amuse me. Somewhere in life, someone told them, "Always be loud. Always. Your conversation is the most important in history, and everybody wants to hear about it." And now they talk loudly at all times. They cannot be on my island at all. I need people who will not talk and just listen as we build a new world.

Last, you eliminate those coughing and sneezing loudly. I cannot have people with low immune systems on my island.

One day as I was playing this odd game in my mind, I observed a woman who literally coughed loudly every five seconds. I wasn't the only one to notice this, and as I boarded the plane I thought, *I pity the person who has to sit next to that lady. Sheesh.* As I settled into my seat and watched the other passengers get on, I could hear the coughing lady coming a mile away. I couldn't wait to see who had the pleasure of riding five hours next to this woman. And to my horror, wouldn't you know that she sat down right next to yours truly.

Almost immediately, the coughing began. As we took off, I felt like the coughs were actually on me. Like an attacking army. About thirty minutes in, I said, "Ma'am, can I please offer you a cough drop? A mint? A face mask? Anything? Because it would seem you're coughing a lot."

She turned to me and said, "I am so sorry. I was afraid this was going to happen. I have lung cancer. I'm flying to see a doctor who hopefully has some answers for me, because I have almost given up hope. And now I'm even destroying people's peaceful flight."

I immediately wanted to jump out of my seat, run to the plane bathroom, and light myself on fire.

I collected myself. I told her that she could cough all she wanted and that I knew people who had fought cancer and won. That I believed in healing and prayer, and that she was a hero, and that if anybody had an issue with her coughing send them to me. We talked almost the entire flight. She even pulled out the X-rays to show me where the cancer was, how bad it had been. And with each detail I felt worse and worse and worse. But also better. Because I knew that once I got off this flight, I would rededicate myself to never taking anything at face value ever again. And this isn't something that I am particularly bad at. But it is something so powerful that it's no surprise it's something we have to keep in focus. Life is actually beautiful. People are fantastic. There is a blessing mixed into anything that could potentially look like a burden.

I have gotten into a habit of saying "I know God is going to use this" when I'm faced with something that seems less than ideal. And what started as a problem ends up being a true blessing. "I have to" is a burden mindset. "I get to" is a blessing mindset. The next time I sit next to somebody who is coughing on a plane, if I think to myself *I have to say something nice because it's my Christian duty*, that becomes an unhealthy burden. If I think to myself *I get to make the best of this, I will find a way to make this productive*, it's hard not to live blessed and fulfilled.

That switch is one we can all make. One of my children said to me on the way to church one Sunday, "Dad, do we *have* to go to church?"

I said, "Absolutely not. But you don't have to eat, either. You don't have to live in this house, matter of fact." I told my son, "We *get* to go to church. This is not a burden, it's our blessing."

It works if you are eight or thirty-eight. This small change leads to a lot of special moments we won't see otherwise.

———————

My challenge for my own life, and for anybody reading this book, is to make a fresh dedication to look deeper. Take a moment at the dinner table, put your phone down, and ask somebody, "How was your day?" And then wait until you actually get an answer, and respond with a follow-up question. In our shallow world, nobody is ready for the follow-up question.

Take a moment at your job and look at the people you work with. Each person has a story. Each person has a dream, a passion. Maybe it's time to try to find out more about them.

If you are in a successful season of life and you are losing the joy in what you wanted so badly, maybe slow down for a moment or two and count the ways you are blessed. Count the ways you are fortunate to be where you are and go remind somebody else that they have awesome things ahead of them as well.

I can almost promise you that your life right this very second has far more gold in it than you may realize. Take every chance you get to stare down the mediocre and the mundane, and refuse to accept it. There are moments to be found, if we can only slow down long enough to see them.

own the chapter

There is always a blessing hidden within what can feel like a burden. What is the most burdensome thing in your life today? Look at that exact thing and make a decision to see it as a help to your life, not a hindrance. Picking up my children from school can often force me to have to rearrange my entire schedule. If I look at it like that. I have chosen to enjoy growing in my creative planning because I get the *honor* of picking up my kids from school while they still want me to. It's a small shift that can change your entire outlook on life. What somebody else is complaining about, I want to be rejoicing about. Choose blessing over burden, wherever you can.

Chapter Eight

Occupy All Streets

"DID YOU FIND THE GOLD in somebody today?"

After I heard my wife, Laura's, phone make that familiar *ping* sound that means she received a text, that was the notice on her screen. I have always believed that Laura is part-woman, part-angel because of her graceful way of handling life and its multiple tasks and her easy, trademark Australian sense of humor that causes her to laugh easily. But this was a new level. While juggling being a full-time mom of three—some would say four because I need Laura more than all three of my children combined—the responsibilities she carries with me as we pastor Hillsong NYC together, and the various unplanned things life throws at all of us, she still is so intentional about helping other people that she sends a reminder to herself to make sure it happens.

"Did you find the gold in somebody today?" What a question.

I know people who may remind themselves to "find the gold today" or even "find somebody" today (as all the single people silently nod their heads right now as they read). But to have a daily life goal to help somebody else just might be the gold rush of a paradigm shift we all need. Because as it stands now? This is not the intent of our culture and not even common wisdom for all those "winning mind-set" books and seminars I see all over the place. That wisdom will tell you to do more, be more, promote more, grind more, hashtag more, and work more . . . for *you*. At times, each one of those things does need to happen. The problem arises when the destination is never defined. What does "more" mean? How much do we actually need in order to finally say, "I made it. I'm a success." If you can't define that, strap on your seat belt really tight because you are on what I like to call the "Highway to Unfulfillment," and although there is carnage, traffic, and frustration on that road, people are still dying to get on it.

I know for a fact there is a better way, a better road, and there is plenty of room on this highway. The only thing required is a true passion to seek a purpose in this life—one in which the person who benefits the most may not be you. But as it turns out, that's exactly the way we end up helping ourselves the most.

I always point people to what I believe is the starting point for actually enjoying the journey in life rather than chasing the ghost that is the destination. Simply realize that who you are will never be defined by what you do. If your worth, your status, and your value are not separated from your vocation or employment definition, it's going to be impossible to deal with the changes that inevitably come at us all in this life. We are so used to giving people value because of a title, we have forgotten that it's *people* who actually give value to titles.

When you know this about yourself internally, it's really easy to be successful and efficient as you perhaps grow into titles and dreams and aspirations that are still in progress. You stop waiting for permission to prosper, you stop waiting for people to give you a voice, and you just start having a voice. You stop waiting for other people to tell you, "It's your time" because you knew the moment you woke, "It's my time, all the time."

I got a golden piece of advice when I was just starting out as a pastor. I was told: "Do not ever wait for other people to tell you that you're ready. Because when you're young, people are going to say, 'You're too young, wait until somebody opens a door.' When you're older, people will say, 'You're too old, wait until there are doors open nobody else chooses.' And you will find yourself looking back saying, 'When was my prime?'"

When I heard that, I started to occupy my street. And by that I mean that whatever I was doing, I was going to do it like it was the last thing I was ever going to do, fully aware and hopeful that it wouldn't be. I wasn't going to get caught up in overlooking what I could do because I was enamored of what I wanted to do next. I wasn't going to go through any motions, because the opportunity right in front of me was worth my time.

You know what happens when you live like that? You stand out. You enjoy life. You become ruthlessly efficient and disciplined—because it all matters. And before you know it, you start stacking little moments like chips at a Vegas casino table and people say things like, "How did you get there?" And you struggle to explain because you just kept working, loving, reaching out, doing what you *can* do rather than lamenting what you *can't* do while watching others do what *they* do.

What if I told you that simply doing what is in your heart right now, even the little decisions, can open up far more doors than you ever realized? It took one lesson from a grieving mother for me to graduate into this life and never look back.

I'm sure you have been there. You catch a fleeting feeling, an idea: Maybe it's to write a song or brainstorm on an idea you have had percolating. But you put it off and think, *I'll get to that, for sure. Later.* Maybe it's even something smaller like that urge to encourage a friend, but you think, *Ah, they are fine. I don't want to bother them.* And you fill your pockets with good intentions until there is no more room.

This used to happen to me all the time. Whether the barrier was fear or busy-ness, I would sense a moment and watch it fly by. Except for the day I had the idea to text Kim Simpson.

Her son Will was a friend of mine. He was in prison for a few years after we'd left high school for some drug-related convictions, but had decided to turn his life around. I remember preaching one night in Virginia Beach and seeing him in about the fourth row. He was in a suit and tie, and although I hadn't seen him in a long time, his face and smile had not changed.

He said, "Carl, I'm going to be here every week. I'm out of jail, finished my rehab. I'm a few months sober and I will sit right here in this row whenever church is open."

We hung out often. I loved hearing his stories and particularly meeting his friends from prison. There is something special about people who appreciate freedom again, and they made me better, more passionate about life. I became one of Will's sponsors. Those familiar with loved ones breaking free from addiction know that this is a high honor: to be on the speed dial for times of trouble or challenge for recovering addicts charts their new life course. And as seriously as I took this role, I missed the one call I needed to answer one night.

I couldn't have known as I turned my phone off that night after a giant day in my own life that a very loud, brand-new screaming baby girl named Ava Angel, having tested each vocal cord for hours before finally shutting it down and going to sleep, that Will would call. I woke up to a phone call from Kim Simpson.

"Can you please come down to the hospital? It's Will."

That night in Virginia Beach, a diabolically made strain of heroin had gone around town and over ten people had died, apparently all purchasing the drug from the same source. One of them was Will. He was on life support when I went in with Kim, but she said they had made peace with what the doctors had said and wanted me to pray for Will as they said goodbye. I won't ever forget putting my hands on his face as we thanked God for his life, and I hugged Kim and almost in a daze wandered out to my car.

I sat there and thought about how I should have called Will. How I would have called him had I known. I'm under no illusions that I am a savior of any sort, and people say well-meaning things in times of crisis, like, "It was out of your control." Sure, that's true to a degree. But it makes zero difference when those unrelenting waves of grief seem to crush your soul as you almost drown in tears after losing somebody you love.

It took me a really long time to forgive myself—and to not *get over* Will passing away but to *get through* it the best I could. I did not know then that I would be in that position many more times in the future. But I chose then to do what I could do, always: Don't *think* about a friend in need. *Call* a friend in need. Not "send good vibes" to those I love but actually call and send words of thanks.

It's impossible to do it all. It's very possible to do a little. And a little adds up.

———————

Five years later, I went to text somebody whose name starts with a *K*, and instead the name *Kim Simpson* came up on the autotype. For whatever reason, my eyes welled up with tears. I had a moment to remember Will, and I thought, *I should text Kim and tell her I love her.*

And then all the normal excuses started to cloud the initial thought:

She's busy.

It's been too long since you texted—it'd be weird now.

It's insensitive to have as little contact as you have had. Just pray for her.

But my own-the-moment-occupy-my-street conviction won out. That's what happens when you lock onto a conviction for long enough. It overrides whatever feeling wants to steer you another way. So I sent the text.

> Kim, I love you. Thinking of you today. I miss Will and I'm grateful that I got to know him and still know you. Have the best day. Love Carl.

Within minutes, she replied back:

> Carl! You have no idea how much this means to me. Today is Will's birthday. He's been gone for a while now. I'm not sure many of his friends even knew his birthday, and I was struggling with the feeling that he is forgotten. This text on this day matters more than you will ever know.

I had no idea. I was elated that in God's grace the timing was so powerful. I was also convicted to my core that there was a good chance that there had been many moments like that which I could have been a part of but I allowed them to slip through my fingers. I revowed, reupped on that day to remember to do what I can do. If a mom who I love found a little bit of gold in the form of a very unspectacular text from a distant friend, how much gold might there be for us to find in life, in others, should we choose to look?

Is there somebody today who you need to call? You should call. Is there somebody who you need to forgive? You should try.

I'm not interested in a person's title. I'm interested in their character.

I'm not interested in "the right place at the right time." I'm focused on "all the time, all the places."

If I'm in it? I'm going to occupy it.

If I have a window? I will open it up, then kick it in so two more people can climb through.

I am not a "preacher." Preaching is what I do. I am a passionate human being who wants to help people, and I just happen to preach right now. But my title will not and cannot determine my tenacity for this calling we call life. All of it. Don't let your title tell you who you are. Your time is now. Today.

Jesus said something to a group of title-less, societal *status*-less people on a hillside one day. He said, "You are the light of the world. If I put you on a hilltop, it's not to hide you. It's so you can shine! So go shine. Live generous lives that open people up to this generous God in heaven." Jesus said nothing about "when you get a title" or "when you know enough" or "when your dream season arrives, activate your gifting." None of that. Jesus knew that what I pray, I now know.

Where I am today? It might not be where I'll be tomorrow. But who I am? That goes with me everywhere I go. I can't control my situation all the time. But I can control my spirit, my faith, my passion. So can you.

Put a reminder on your phone tonight that will show up tomorrow. Have it say: "Did you find the gold in somebody today?"

own the chapter

What have you been waiting for that you actually don't have to wait for? Influence and significance are not found in position or title. They're found in passion and intentional living. My pastor taught me long ago to intend to fulfill what is in my heart. Meaning, don't fulfill what is in my heart because you are always focusing on what you don't have. What can you do *today*? Who can you reach *today*? Occupy your street today with passion, and it will undoubtedly lead to a highway of opportunity.

Chapter Nine

Your Security Is Your Serenity

AT SOME POINT, WE ALL have to take a really long look at where our security comes from. Insecurity has been the ultimate root of so many breakdowns—from relationships to dreams to taking giant steps of faith—that it should be listed among the world's most deadly things. Right up there with virtually every animal in Australia.

I think the security journey is one that nobody will ever fully master or conquer this side of eternity. However, I do believe there is something to be said for those of us who are not willing to settle for at best a "shaky" security system. Surely there is a better option for us in this life than finding our worth, finding our value, finding our status in things, titles, and popularity. I believe there absolutely is, and in a culture that literally promotes concepts and thinking around this subject that have been proven time and time again to not work, maybe it's time to own this issue outright and start to look at the way we build our security and our self-esteem.

The sad truth is that insecurity is so obvious. We might as well handle it because everybody else can see it anyway. Insecurity is *loud*. Living in New York, you see this often. The guys who walk into a room and announce themselves, promote themselves, and continue to talk about themselves are dead giveaways for people who actually don't have that much going on. Security gives you the peace to not perform. To not promote. It's the guy smiling in the back of the room, listening to the other guy talk about how great his office is, who probably owns the building that guy's office is in. Insecurity keeps you talking, because you are afraid of what the "silence" might actually expose. If you're good at something, it's going to show. Truly secure people thrive in the shadows because they know their time is going to come.

One of my friends who is a true New Yorker was educating me on the NYC drug trade. As an avid fan of the show *The*

Wire,[1] I can't hear enough about this fascinating and deadly profession that still has a huge grip on my city and so many others. We were in Harlem for a basketball game, and a guy drove up in a car that was worth at least $100K. He was dripping in jewelry and, from the color of his outfit, was very proud of his gang affiliation. I said to my friend that this guy "was probably a big deal." My friend gave me the very astute observation that, in fact, he wasn't a big deal at all. He said the real kingpins in this city drive rental cars. The lower the profile, the higher the efficiency. And yes, I am a preacher and will spin anything into a sermon. But the connection to application here is a screaming red light. At some point we have to rest in who we are and let our efficiency do the talking.

If you are great, you don't have to tell everybody that you are great. Your work will prove that. Your character will outline that and do the talking for you. You don't have to top every story in every conversation to make sure everybody knows that yes, you too have done interesting things. You can happily and readily cheer for others when they win without finding ways to discredit what they did, to make yourself feel better about where you stand.

True security can make you a phenomenal cheerleader.

---

[1] If you don't like that show, we can't be friends. Ever.

You can do something for somebody without making sure there is a way for what you did to be reciprocated. Because you can do things with genuine motives when you're secure that insecure people cannot. It's love without conditions because there is no competition. Security breeds and produces more security. If you don't have it, you need to find it quick because it can become one of the biggest strengths in your life.

Another friend of mine used to embody this issue to the fullest. Although he had established a career in the fashion world on both sides of the camera as a designer and a model, his security level did not match his success level. Yet as we know from the body dysmorphia example earlier, people sometimes struggle to see themselves for who they really are. So he always made it a point to tell everyone how many people thought he was handsome. He would say, "Man, I walked down the street today and at least five girls stopped me and asked me for my number." Any time somebody else would get a win, he would find a way to talk about a bigger win for himself. If you just won a free vacation? Trust me, this guy would find a way to talk about a free island he'd won. We all know these people.

One day I'd simply had enough, and asked him if he understood that the louder he talked, the less people actually believed what he said. I wondered if he knew that at some point he could rest in the fact that we all thought he was awesome and we loved him *for him.*

The truth came out that day. About how his whole life had been a struggle to prove people wrong. That nobody ever helped him, so he couldn't break the habit of making sure he helped himself.

This is not peace. This is the constant pressure that insecurity brings. Do you find yourself being too loud about yourself? It may be time to turn a page in your story of security. If you are not secure in who you are, you will spend the rest of your life listening to other people tell you about you, and they should not have that right.

Because I am a Christian, I believe my journey to security should be far more progressive than people who are uncertain about where they came from, and why they are here, or if there is a God at all. Not only do I believe in God, I believe God created me, Jesus saved me, and His hand continues to guide me regardless of my "performance" in this life.

I have zero excuse for functioning out of an insecure position. If I lost my job, nobody knew my name, and nobody ever patted me on the back again and said, "You're doing great," I'm sure it wouldn't be easy. But my prayer is that my security in who I am will always be stronger than my security in what I do.

One of these is absolutely uncontrollable. Economic collapse, cultural shifts, and general calamities and tragedies that spare none of us are vivid pieces of evidence that prove the case that what we do in this life will change. Yet our propensity to put our faith in things that have no promise of permanency is way too high. Often people start so far behind on this subject due to how they were raised and the people they grew up around. I can't count how many times I have heard heartbreaking stories of people opening up about a parent who planted a negative seed of doubt, a well-founded fear that somebody would let them down again, as had happened so many times before. Sometimes our insecurities are actually based around real factors.

But I still believe these are challenges we can overcome. If you can't take big risks, if you can't step out into new things freely, if you can't give away what you have quickly and readily because you're not certain you can get more? Then you have insecurity issues that are affecting your ability to create true change in this world. I want to be a leader and a husband and a pastor who is so secure that I can love quickly, give generously, and forgive freely because I know where my life is anchored.

Recently my father-in-law—who happens to be one of the most secure and life-loving Australian legends you could ever meet—gave my daughter Charlie seventy dollars "just because." I don't care how rich you are, seventy dollars is awesome. And when you are ten, it's a bonanza.

So I did what I always do when my children get money: I told her to give it to me because I gave her *life* and she owes me. No, I told her to make sure she saved a portion of it to give at church the following week. The principle in action here is remembering where your source is, because if you can't give it away, you never really had it anyway. Laura and I made a decision a long time ago to at least give 10 percent of what we make to the church that we are committed to. So naturally it was Charlie's idea to give 10 percent. I told her to pray about it, decide what she wanted to give out of her amazing financial windfall, and tell me on Sunday.

I had forgotten about it, and that day I got up to lead a church meeting when I felt a little tug on my leg. It was Charlie holding an envelope. She said, "Dad, here is my offering." I quickly checked to see the details on this envelope because in the past my children have given—on my behalf—my money, without me knowing.

Once I verified this wasn't the case, I said, "How much are you gonna give?"

She said, "All seventy, Dad."

I said, "Girl! That is so sweet. But you don't have to do that. Seven dollars is totally sufficient."

She proceeded to tell me, "Dad, it's fine. I want to give it all. And if I need more? I will just ask you!"

Please believe that after I was done crying, the ATM could not stop me from withdrawing as much money as I could to fill her little generous pockets. I was convinced that this little human had so much faith and security in her daddy that she could already give everything she had with zero fear that her needs would not be met.

This is true security. I will give away my best ideas. Because I know where to find more. I will encourage everybody I see. Because I myself am encouraged. I will highlight and celebrate others. Because I know internally where my worth and my esteem come from. If you don't live like this, then you can and you should.

When we begin to own our insecurity, I think so much in this world begins to open up. A closed fist is a bad recipient. An open hand can hold so much more. There is more peace for you in your life than you realize. The question will be: How much do you want?

My challenge to you is to face down one area of insecurity in your life. Do the exact opposite of what your fear tells you to do. Day by day, that fear will lose its grip on you, and you will start to get a glimpse of the *free* you.

own the chapter

What makes you the most insecure in life? Is it the success of others? Is it people who are doing what you want to do someday but you can't do currently? Is it constant comparison to people and things that are not even running the same race as you? Do the exact opposite of what insecurity tells you to do. Cheer for somebody who is winning when you're tempted to tear them down. Reach out to the person who you wish would reach out to you. When comparison creeps in, remind yourself that you are content simply being you. Insecurity's grip on your life is not as tight as you may imagine.

Chapter Ten

Living the Dream

"LENTZ! IS THAT YOU?"

I heard my old friend from across the bar and realized it had been a very long time since we had seen each other. He and another guy began making their way through the crowd to say hello in that unmistakable way that lets everybody know they had been drinking for a while. It's not quite a stumble, definitely not a sprint. More of an "intoxicated float" that makes me laugh every time.

I hadn't been home to Virginia Beach for quite some time after I had become a Christian. I went across the world for Bible college and began working in a church. I had heard some solid rumors about myself by that time: I worked for the Peace

Corps. I went on a mission trip to the Congo and never came back. I joined a cult. All of that was fine with me because I've learned that if people are not talking about you, it's because you're not making much of a difference. But I didn't realize just how "mysterious" my choices had become until this conversation.

My old friend said, "Carl! What on Earth have you been doing? I heard you became a priest. Why would you do that?"

I assured him that no, in fact, I had not become a priest but a pastor—and I explained the giant difference between the two.

"Well, that still sounds awful," he said. "Let me tell you what *I* have been up to. I make more money than I can count. I have a steady girlfriend, but I have about ten 'unsteady' chicks on the side, if you know what I mean. I'm not tied down to anybody. I have a real job *and* a job the government doesn't know about and still haven't got caught. I can walk into any spot in town and everybody knows me. I have been living the dream!"

I sat there and listened to my friend talk for a while and politely nodded, but as I left I couldn't help but think how much his "dream" life sounded like a nightmare to me. And how awfully close I had been to attempting to live that very same dream before I decided to shift course and pursue not "the dream" but a reality—one that I am so present in, I no longer look or long for a scenario that most likely will never come.

That's the thing about misguided dreaming: There is a huge chance you can overlook the reality and opportunity that are right in front of you. This entire book—and, honestly, my brief thirty-eight years on this Earth—could be summed up like this: I want to live so well, so present, so passionate, so purposeful, that what I used to dream about is disappointing.

I am in no way "anti-dream." I am, however, a huge proponent of making sure that if my head is in the clouds dreaming, my feet had better be moving on the ground. Perhaps one of the most moving sermons or public speeches of the modern era was given by Martin Luther King Jr., who declared, "I have a dream . . ." What made that special, however, was that he also had a progressive daily life that continually put him in a position to walk toward that dream. I'm not going to wait for some scenario to happen where I say, "Yes. My dream. Now it's time to thrive." I think we can cultivate a reality by design that we find fulfillment in. But perhaps it starts with "changing the dream." Or maybe it's even time to let the dream "go"— so it doesn't take up space in your heart and mind that could be filled with something even better. Some might scoff at my friend in the bar, thinking, *That guy has a bad idea of what the dream life is.* Possibly true. But I think we *all* have a bad idea of what the dream life is if it means we see it only when we sleep.

My dream church? It's the one I pastor, right now. My dream house? I'm sleeping in it. I'm sure it won't be the last one, and I have some ideas about what the future can hold, without a doubt. But I'm not going to walk around with that feeling all the time that gnaws slowly at so many: that feeling that says, "There has to be something better." That's like looking at a baby in a crib and never holding it, never laughing when they laugh, never tapping them on the nose and hearing those heavenly baby laughs as they figure out the rhythm of their own voice and yours. Instead, you look at the crib every day and go, "Someday, that's going to be an amazing human. I'll check back next year." Sometimes we have to learn how to not look so far ahead we miss the fact that what we have is worth looking at.

———

I think I am over my tattoo phase, but if I did add something it would be *DREAM BIG BUT LIVE BETTER.* That's essentially what the scripture says in Ephesians 3:20: God "is able to do immeasurably more than all we ask or imagine according to His power that is at work in us, to Him be glory . . ." That passage opens my eyes every day to the power of right now. Because if this is true—and I believe it is with my whole heart—my dreams are fantastic. But God is so good that He will exceed them anyway, rewrite them better, so I might as well live like what I'm doing *is* the dream, because there is probably more in it than I realize.

I never "dreamed" I would be a pastor. Ever. I never would have picked this life. But I'm glad God doesn't always take my dream orders, like a waiter in a Brooklyn diner. Because I found out what I was born to do on the run. In the fight. And I've heard other people tell this exact same story.

I received a letter one day from Seattle, Washington, that would forever solidify this thought in my life. I had preached there a couple weeks prior, and I could feel on that night that people were getting the idea. When you're a preacher, you can feel sometimes whether what you're saying is just entering people's heads or if it's actually impacting their hearts. If it's the latter, sometimes the feedback in the moment is quieter, but you know people are registering the information on a different level. That's how I felt after that night. The letter read:

> *I really appreciated the message about doing what I can right now, and not waiting for the perfect time and perfect season. I have always thought that someday I would be in ministry,*

preaching. In a church. So my current occupation as a police officer has been great, but I always thought perhaps it was a precursor. As you preached, I realized that there is no need to wait. That I can live some of that dream in my everyday life. So I began to work differently. Typically when we make arrests, we put the person in the back of the car and drive them to the station in relative silence. But I started playing videos of preaching that I love, sometimes your sermons, for them to watch on the way while handcuffed. I figured, "Where else are they gonna go?"[1] Often they would ask me to pray for them, to keep them in mind as they deal with the consequences of their actions, and I am able to always tell them to never forget that the grace of God is always available no matter what we have done. Some of these people have even tracked me down upon their prison release and asked to come to church for more information on that sermon they heard. So thank you for helping me see that, yes, I have a bright future. But my "right now" is pretty amazing. I'm a preaching police officer that pastors perpetrators.

That does not sound like a dream to me. It sounds way better. That man has become a close friend of mine, and over the years I have seen him get promotion after promotion to where he sits now, as a premier agent in his department. But

[1]This, my friends, is what I call a captive audience.

that's what happens when we kill the dream sometimes. Reality has no choice but to get brighter because our attention is on it.

It's far easier to do than you may think. Start tomorrow by being grateful it started at all. Pick the most ordinary thing you do and make a conscious decision to put passion into it and see what happens. This is by no means a magic elixir that guarantees endless promotion and power. But it is a surefire way to not neglect the things you can do right now.

I was asked recently, "Are you living the dream? It looks like it." I answered, respectfully, "No. I killed the dream. I'm living something better. A reality that I can feel, and share, and pass on."

I don't see my dreams when I close my eyes. I think we can live something greater when we truly open them.

own the chapter

Every dream ends the same way. You wake up. "Stay woke" has become a trendy term for those who want to remain aware about cultural issues, injustice, and anything that demands immediate attention. Perhaps it gets overlooked when it comes to applying it to our own lives, our own opportunities. Today is a fantastic day to wake up and start impacting people in your everyday world. Since no "dream" comes to pass in a single day anyway, you might as well enjoy the journey as you wait for something to come to pass. Who knows? If you wake up to the realities in your life, maybe you will stumble upon something you didn't even know you were passionate about. What was the pursuit of one dream can become the reality of living out many opportunities if you choose to awaken to all the possibilities God has placed in your path.

Chapter Eleven

If Jesus Had Instagram

I LIKE SOCIAL MEDIA. THE benefits and the connectivity and the ability to stay up to date with people, events, and causes far outweigh the minor annoyances of the occasional troll or negative news you may come across. I particularly like Instagram, because I am a visual learner: I like writing and reading captions that help give context to images that matter to people.

One of the challenges of Instagram, though, is that sometimes we can see a photo or an image and have no idea what led to that photo or image. The road navigated, the story behind it, the factors that were in play, perhaps even the ninety-seven filters not chosen to cast just that right amount of color on a dark corner. To a degree, it's not that big a deal. Unless people get enamored with almost a "mythical" destination that does not really exist. You see somebody post a photo of a car? *Oh, I want that car.* Perhaps you don't see the bike they rode for years in less fortunate times. You see a post of somebody leading a meeting of high-level staff in a business setting with the hashtag "#corporateceolife" and think, *I want to be a boss too.* Yet you don't see all the coffee runs they made when they were a lowly assistant.

In my world as a pastor this issue is prevalent because, whether people admit it or not, you see what other people are doing and it can create unhealthy comparisons and frustrations that are unneeded. If you're a pastor and you follow somebody who is seemingly preaching to thousands of people all the time, and every service looks like it's packed beyond capacity, you can go back to your world and struggle with your actual reality. The problem is that nobody just shows up at these successful photo moments. And furthermore, very few people actually Instagram their bad days. I have yet to see a pastor's Instagram photo with the caption: "Here I am. Looks like 80 percent of the people I lead decided not to show."

Maybe if they did, that would actually help the cause. When we choose to take ownership of what we can do in this life and stay faithful and passionate about it day in and day out, it absolutely will at some point link to another moment.

And then another. And then another. And then someday you find yourself in a position of strength or growth, and people will start asking, "When was your big break? What was 'the moment'?" You will be able to explain to them that you actually don't know when your big moment was, because you had just been faithfully building what was in front of you and then looked up one day and didn't even realize all the ground you had covered.

I love "big break" stories. And they do make for incredible movies. But when I study my heroes and even look at my own journey? I realize that what somebody is "known for" almost pales in comparison to what they did to actually get there.

Most people would immediately associate Jesus Christ with a cross. For better or for worse, with context or without, most people at least know that Jesus died on that cross. If that's all anybody ever heard, it's important enough and life-changing enough on its own. But what gets me about Jesus—and what makes the "Instagram" of Him hanging on a cross, that particular destination, even more amazing—is the road that led Him there.

I often wonder: What if Jesus had Instagram? How awesome would that have been? Obviously his handle would've been @therealking. "Here I am. Floating. Chilling. #floachilling."

But I wonder if people would have followed Him. Because, yes, in hindsight we believe some amazing things were happening. But in the moment they probably looked pretty ordinary. Sometimes the Gospel accounts of Jesus can play out like a *SportsCenter* highlight reel, but in truth, Jesus was fully human. He would have had days that look just like many of our days. The difference is that each moment He lived, each person He met, was actually playing a part in the greater story.

One moment in particular still to this day moves me each time I read it. Jesus was being followed by tons of people. Not Instagram followed but literally followed around. People were enamored by His life, the miracles they were seeing, and the questions he was producing. And one day as He was headed somewhere He stopped, looked up in a tree, and spoke to a man who had climbed up there to get a better glimpse of Him.

The man's name was Zacchaeus, and he was a notorious, reviled man. Most would steer clear of him. Yet Jesus, eyes wide open, not only talked to him but ended up going to dinner with him. This broke common-barrier rules. Not to mention, dinner in this day and age was not for a moment. It was most likely a production that would have taken a very long time. I don't know what Jesus's plans were prior to seeing Zacchaeus in that tree, but He altered them. The result: Zacchaeus was so impacted by Jesus that at the dinner he stood up and pronounced: "Look, Lord! Here and now I give half of my possessions to the poor, and if I have cheated anybody out of anything, I will pay back four times the amount." That must have been a moment. I wonder what Jesus talked about. What jokes He told. What segues He would have used. Something happened at that table, and the end result was a man going from death to life. My takeaway from this story? Maybe I need to tolerate more interruptions in my life. Maybe I wouldn't choose a particular course of events that transpire in my life, but if I keep my eyes open, I can still make the best of even unwanted moments.

Back to the Instagram parallel for a moment: Most of this encounter would have been unspectacular. It was obviously inconvenient. It would have been widely misunderstood, as Jesus was at the wrong place with the wrong people at the wrong time in culture, according to many. By the way, if Jesus did have an Instagram, I have to believe that in the comment section He would have had the best clap backs of all time. "Jesus, how dare you hang out with such bad people? You are terrible. I write this out of love. From @logineye." Jesus's response: "I am God." Surely He would have used that each time. But there would not be a wasted moment. I think we have so many moments in our lives that, if we allow frustration or fatigue to minimize them, almost like a "this moment isn't even worthy of a photo" mentality, there is no way we can effectively do or be who we are called to be. Just because our days at times look unspectacular doesn't mean that something supernatural is not around the corner.

But after reading about stories like Jesus and Zacchaeus and so, so many more, when you finally do explore Jesus to the point it leads you to the cross? That one photo, that one moment means even more. That cross wasn't just for the known, or the cool, or the followers. It was for the people in the trees.

Even when something big has happened, I have always been conscious of how many little factors played a role in getting me in a position to walk through that open door. But that big open door has never been my goal. I have been content my whole life to make peace with even the crack of an "opportunity window," while other people I have known are waiting anxiously for the big door of opportunity. I have never had time for that, and I have realized over time that sometimes the open window is a better place from which to enter a giant house of opportunity anyway.

I spoke to a young up-and-coming leader once who was peppering me with questions about how to grow his church. He was asking me if there were certain themes I do, if there were "methods" that help us always stay on the front lines and make sure we don't get complacent or stagnant with what we have. And I told him I honestly couldn't name one, other than this: "Keep your eyes open when you're at 7-Eleven."

When I first began as a preacher in Virginia Beach,[1] we led a really small movement that I felt had the potential to grow. And we didn't have big teams or big ideas, so I just figured that I would personally do my best to ask every individual I came across if they wanted to come to church. I even asked a police officer once, after he wrote me a ticket, if he would be my guest. He declined and thought I was weird. Win some, lose some.

But this type of thinking led me to always be looking, listening. Because I knew if I reached one person, that person would reach at least one more. And one way or another, we were gonna get this word out.

I was late for church one Sunday. And as I stopped to get my customary coffee and Krispy Kreme doughnut—which I have since found out for sure are made in actual Heaven—I rushed to the register to pay. I pulled out my money, got busy on a text, and as I walked out I realized the man behind the

---

[1]Shout-out to the 757—the greatest area code of all time! Teddy Riley, Pharrell Williams, Missy Misdemeanor Elliot, Chad Hugo, Kenna Zemedkun, Charles Park, Allen Iverson, James McAdoo, No Malice and Pusha T—my favorite rap duo ever. WE INVENTED HIP-HOP AND BASKETBALL. TWO UP, TWO DOWN, TO ALL OF YOU.

counter had said, "Where are you headed?" So I went back and apologized for not hearing him right away.

"I am headed to church," I said. "You would love my church. Do you want to come?"

He looked at me and said, "I am not a church guy. I do not do church."

I've done this long enough to know that some people say things hoping to get more conversation and others say things hoping to end it. This was the latter.

I looked at his nametag.

"Well, Ross," I said, "I go to a church full of people who don't really like church either. So we have built this church in such a way that church isn't really the thing. Jesus is the main thing. And you need to come."

He thought about it for a second and said, "Okay, I will give it a shot."

Later that night, he followed through. I saved him a seat, and he came to sit there—in his 7-Eleven gear, nametag and all.

That night Ross's life changed. He called me the next week, and he said, "If it's okay, I would like to bring my wife."

And I told him, "No, Ross. Around here we only accept half a couple until we know you're serious. Of course you can bring her!" Ross's wife came that day. Her life was profoundly impacted, and I had made yet another friend.

The next week, Ross called me again and said, "So my daughter from another marriage wants to come with five of her friends. Can they come?"

I said, "Ross, you have got to stop asking me if people can come. Literally anybody you can get in here is welcome."

Within one month, I was saving over five rows of seats for Ross and his people. Before long, those rows turned into more rows. I looked out one time during church and saw a few of these faces and thought to myself, "Thank Heaven for 7-Eleven."

I have since come to realize that this works in every area of my entire life. I no longer look for big opportunities. I no longer hope I just stumble upon some magical, perfect scenario that will make everything okay. If I can own the moment directly in front of me, do my absolute best to stay faithful to it, I can be at peace regardless of what comes next. I don't have control of what comes next to a large degree in this life, but I do have control of what moments, what people, what opportunities I have right now.

My challenge for you is this: Take a moment today, this week, and refuse to allow anything to be "just another." Just another day at the office. Just another trip to the store with my daughter. Just another story I have to read to my kid before he goes to sleep. Just another text to my wife telling her I'm on my way home.

No! It's not "just another." Make it the best story you have ever read. Make it the most amazing, engaging subway ride you have ever been on. Make it the most heartfelt, romantic text you have ever sent. You'd better believe that last one will lead to something greater. And the other ones will too.

Keep your eyes open in this 7-Eleven we call life. Don't let days or seasons when you feel like you are in constant shadow rob you of the reality that sunlight is truly on the way. Sometimes there are days when nobody else is going to believe your life is headed in the right direction. As long as you believe it? Let them think what they want. You get to choose what kind of day, what kind of attitude you're going to have.

My daughter Charlie took an epic photo of a sunset one afternoon. I have reluctantly allowed her to have an Instagram because she is so creative, and I want her to be able to express herself and not be scared of the big bad world of online anything. Plus, I control who follows her, and it's a short list. But I saw the look on her face as she was staring at the photo she took, and she said, "Dad, I want to post it, because I like it. But what if nobody else likes it?"

I said, "Girl, you better post that picture. Right now. Because *you* like it. If other people like it, great. But don't ever let that stop you from enjoying something. Even if you are the only one who sees what you see."

She posted it, but I learned from it. I thought about moments in my life that perhaps I have not fully embraced, or that maybe I endured rather than enjoyed, because I was concerned about the way somebody else would see them. Wondering whether they would like them. If they would understand them. I have resolved to embrace what I can, when I can. And sometimes, the photos or days that other people don't love? Those end up being the ones I love the most. Beauty—even significance—appears to still lie with the beholder.

own the chapter

One of the best ways to make it through "your process" as you grow and gain ground in your own life is making sure somebody else is involved. Serving somebody else, giving lessons from your journey and getting your eyes off your own circumstance is perhaps the most underrated way to refuel your own soul. What starts out as a service and blessing for another becomes something that ends up helping you far more than it helps them. If you are always the star in your story, it becomes a very dull narrative. Might be time to make room for others.

Chapter Twelve

I Have No Idea Where I'm Going

FINDING DIRECTION IN THIS LIFE is not easy. If it was, there would not be so many options, methods, and seminars full of answers to this very topic. I still find it very funny that the two questions most typed into Google are "Is Tupac dead?"[1] followed by "Why am I here?" When it comes to the latter, there is not a person on Earth who has not contemplated this at least one million times. Some of us hit that total within a week.

---

[1] I'm not satisfied with any of the conspiracy theories I have heard—though when Snoop Dogg rolled out that hologram a few years back at Coachella it was a little *too* real.

One of the challenges to finding these crucial and important answers is that the presence of many answers doesn't equate to any of them actually being *right*. In fact, you can always go find somebody who will tell you exactly what you want to hear. Want to be a vegan? You can find countless blogs and websites detailing exactly why you should never touch meat again. How being a vegan will drastically improve your quality of life. How crazy it is to not know this. Hate eating plants? You can find an equal number of blogs and websites dedicated to tearing down every argument a vegan ever produced. Want to raise your children without spanking them? You can join a club that promotes parental diplomacy and giving your child "options" and feel totally fine when your kid tells you what to do instead of vice versa, because that's what diplomacy is all about. If you want a divorce, you can go find people who will tell you marriage is an antiquated social construct anyway, and that monogamy is an insane proposition in the first place, and that people fall in and out of love all the time, and that you can't live bound to one chapter of love when there is a whole book in front of you. And off to divorce court you go. Conversely, you can go talk to a marriage counselor or somebody like me who's probably gonna give you wisdom in the direction of "Let's look in before you look out. Most marriage difficulties are overcome-able, and it includes a lot of sacrifice and servanthood." Or, "Hey, nobody falls in or out of love.

That is a Hollywood construct. We choose to love, and we choose to stop loving. So don't put this on your feelings—own your choice."[2]

Our world is now ingrained to not look for direction but to look for comfort—what suits our desire the most. And often this comes at the expense of true guidance. That's why who you hear from matters so very much.

We need to be voraciously vigilant about where we get our information from and who we get it from, or else we might look back someday and realize we have poured blood, sweat, and far too many tears into a direction or cause or passion that actually had zero impact on people and the world we are called to change.

Because I am a follower of Jesus, I have a giant example that essentially makes it impossible for me to miss my purpose. My purpose in life is to live like Jesus, talk like Jesus, treat people like Jesus did, have compassion like Jesus did, love people like Jesus did. What I actually do for a living is secondary to who I am and where I am headed. That is an important distinction to

---

[2]By the way, if you want to be an unpopular source for wisdom, frequently use these buzzwords and phrases: *sacrifice*, *it's not about you*, *die to yourself*, *honor your vows*, *look in the mirror*. These will buy you some peace and quiet.

make in this life. Often what we do will not match who we are. Your job or label might be undervalued by some. But if you know where you are headed, if you know why you are here, you end up bringing value to your vocation rather than vice versa.

This perspective I have comes from wisdom, not chance. I saw a friend of mine recently looking over his horoscope in the local paper. Now, if you are a big believer in horoscopes, you do you. I happen to be a person who believes I can talk to God, the *creator* of the stars, rather than somebody telling me what my star sign is. My friend said, "This is my month to really make a difference. I am a Scorpio." To which I said, "Wow. You better get to work, because I thought the Age of Aquarius was upon us. Your window might be really limited." If my direction in life is based on my star sign, I'm just going to pack it in now.

I want to make the most of my days, and I think getting control of our directional capabilities is easier than we may think. Best place to start? Have a long look at what information you have gathered about you, about your life, and who gave it to you. Are these people *for* you? Do they want what's best for you? Sometimes simply aligning yourself with people who have done what you want to do, who have actually successfully navigated some of life's most commonly found land mines, is so helpful.

For instance, many of us have the knowledge that smoking will absolutely kill you and destroy your body. Yet you can find millions of knowledgeable adults smoking. I smoked my first cigarette when I was fourteen years old. I knew it was bad, and I knew it was unhealthy. Many cigarettes and way too many years later, I finally had the wisdom to actually quit smoking. Knowledge can lead you to the door. Wisdom opens it and walks you through it.

We all need wisdom in this life. It's vastly different from knowledge. Knowledge is facts or information gathered through experience. Wisdom is knowledge applied. You can gain knowledge in a classroom. Cool. I want to hear from people who have wisdom. Where they actually *did* it. There is a reason why there are so few effective communicators in churches and seminars everywhere: Most of the time people learn how to preach from a professor in a classroom. I learned how to preach from a preacher who preaches. Let somebody take you and show you places you can't go on your own.

———

When I first moved to New York City, it was a directional trial by fire. Growing up in Virginia, I grew accustomed to certain things like civility, road rules, streets that made sense. New York? When you first land here, unless you are like a cartographer by nature, it's confusing.

To compound issues, I took the subway everywhere. For anybody who has had this pleasure, most trains are designated by letter, and you have to sometimes get on multiple trains to get to your destination. If you get lost and ask somebody for help, most New Yorkers are cool but also in a hurry. So the way they explain things is almost like an old school hip-hop song: "You gotta take the 1 to the L to the F to the Q to the 7." And you just go, "Oh, totally." And continue on your ill-fated journey.

On one particularly frustrating, hot summer day, I got off at the wrong stop—again—and thought, *You know what? Let me take a break and sit for a moment and gather my thoughts.* So I sat down on what I thought was a random box.

A woman came up to me and she said, "Baby, you lost? You okay? Where you from?"

I said, "Well, matter of fact, I am lost, and I'm not from around here. What gave me away?"

She said, "Well, for one, you are sitting on a rat trap."

I looked down and realized that, yes, in fact I was on a portable home for the most disgusting NYC creation of all time, evidenced by a giant tail belonging to a very dead NYC rat. This kind lady took me by the hand, walked me to a giant map, and slowly and clearly pointed out exactly where I needed to go, how fast the trains change and switch, and where not to sit in case it's so packed. She even hugged me.

From that day, I was much clearer and much more efficient on these subways. I still missed a stop or two, but I felt more confident. And not long after, I was even giving sage advice to other bewildered people in the concrete jungle.

Sometimes in this life, you need to be humble enough, willing enough to allow people to call you out and steer you right. That day I could have played it cool, pretended that I had meant to sit on a rat trap, and continued an unwanted tour of the five boroughs. But I'm glad I didn't.

I can't tell you how many people I have come across, prayed with, counseled in this life who are headed in a direction they do not have to go. Almost always, they are operating under bad direction. "Somebody told me . . ." "My parents said . . ." "This is what I can expect in life . . ." If you are one of the lucky ones like me who had parents who were kind and amazing and full of wisdom, you can skip ahead. But if you are not? Ask yourself how you came to the conclusions you have. What direction are your relationships headed in? Do you love where your career is headed? Are you happy with the trail you leave behind in this life? Proud of the direction you are leaving for others who are going to come behind you?

If you answered no to any of these questions, it's not too late. It starts by seeking truth. You may have to dig deep into who you *were* to actually find out who you *are* and who you can *become*.

I talked to a friend who was on the brink of divorce once. He said, "I mean, it's no surprise. This is how it's always been for men in my family." I immediately asked him to name his source of information, so I could call them and let them know their help was no longer wanted and we refused to head in that direction. Is your life headed anywhere you don't want it to go? Then put your hand up. Seek some wisdom. And when you do, be prepared to hear what you perhaps don't want to hear but need to. Not only will it drastically help *your* life, but it has the potential to shape those who will follow you someday.

own the chapter

Do you know where you are headed? Maybe the more important question is: Do you know who sent you? Because if you trust the "who," the "where" is far more bearable when you face seasons of uncertainty. Purpose is more than a job or a scenario that you think is right for you. Living with purpose is a mentality. We can achieve our purpose in any scenario if we trust the plan and who created the plan in the first place. There is no better time than now to own some of the hardest questions in life. Why are you here? Where do you find joy and passion in this life and how can you do more of that? One thing is for certain: Avoiding these questions creates more pressure and less peace. God didn't put you on this earth to merely exist and vanish. Live with purpose, on purpose. Every single day.

Chapter Thirteen

The Walking Dead

IT IS A GOOD FEELING to be able to say, "I was there." When you hear people talking about an event, something memorable and epic—it's like a weird badge of honor that perhaps nobody really cares about but you, yet it is still really satisfying.

I remember, as a kid, my mom and dad passionately sharing firsthand accounts of memories and experiences, and they would fly right over my head for the most part. "Son, I remember your first day of school!" Oh, yay. Good for you, Mom. I'm sure it was fantastic. But the older I get, the more I get it. That time is fleeting, our culture is moving extremely fast, and some things in this life you have to literally hold on to, savor, and cherish, because "being present" just might be the most valuable state of being in our lives.

It's one thing to be "around" something; but to be in it and to live it changes how you feel about it drastically. One thing is for certain: I do not want to sleepwalk through this life. We all know that feeling where you wake up late because you have a love affair with the snooze button. And then you proceed to rush your entire routine, leaving the house when you're half awake, and everybody knows it: Your outfit doesn't match, your hair is disheveled, you look sleepy. And you have to fake your way through a meeting or two, all the while knowing everybody else probably knows: *This guy just woke up.*

I remember leaving my house one time for the airport really early in the morning, and I couldn't shake the feeling I had forgotten something—only to realize about a mile into my trip that I had forgotten my shoes. It's also a reason why the show *The Walking Dead* is such a cultural phenomenon. Because people relate to the zombies, aimlessly wandering from thing to thing.

———

I especially feel like this as a parent sometimes, being so caught up in providing for and parenting my kids that I sometimes worry if I'm spending enough time actually enjoying these little people. And I try to fight it, to varying degrees of success.

Recently my wife informed me that one of our daughters had a school dance recital at . . . wait for it . . . eight o'clock on a Tuesday morning! I would love to find out what weird little parent meeting went down where people planned that. "Let's see how we can make dance recitals even worse for parents. Let's do it in the morning, before school, on a Tuesday."

Laura knows my propensity to sleep in, rush around, and be half present, so she warned/threatened me that I needed to be ready and present so I wouldn't miss it. Sure enough, I slept in, barely made it, stumbled into the back of the auditorium while still eating my breakfast, and literally don't recall a single thing that happened. Keep in mind, more responsible parents were there early, eager to film this epic event on their various cameras to rush home and upload said video to a Facebook account that nobody will ever view. But my wife has photographic evidence of just how bad *I* looked at this moment.

Later in the day I panicked when I realized that my daughter Charlie would surely be asking me exactly which part of her twenty-second routine I loved the most, to which I would have to creatively manufacture this memory. I gathered Laura's video of the dance, looked at photos she had taken, and had to diligently work at pretending I remembered an event I actually attended. It worked.[1] But I missed out on the power of the moment.

———————

This to me is our challenge as humans. I do not want to be so fixed on the future that I miss the power of the present. I do not want to be so motivated on what is next that I miss the joy right here, right now. And I know that it's possible to maximize the days, the hidden moments. The parts of the journey that seem mundane to many can be mesmerizing to me.

I was once told that people often do not need a position change, they need a perspective change. It is as true as the day is long. I don't even think that positional happiness is an achievable goal, anyway. Because wherever you go, there you are. So we either learn how to live with vision and simultaneously cultivate extreme contentment in who we are and what we do have; or we spend the rest of our days looking for something that we have the power to possess innately. I want the former. And I think you should too.

I would propose that we have far more beauty, far more opportunity, than we realize. And it's time to live that life. I

[1]Charlie, if you are reading this: I love you, and this is the only time it's happened, and I will make sure it never happens again to the best of my ability, and I will make this up to you and buy you a pony if this wound is still fresh.

don't want life to happen to me; I want to happen to life. I don't want my situation to define me; I want to define my situation. I want to be like one of my friends and heroes, Arlene.

I got a call from her late one Saturday night. One of our strengths as a church family is we do whatever we can to invite and reach out to whoever we can. Often I will get dozens of texts from people asking if they can save seats, if I can sneak somebody in if the building is at max capacity. So Arlene asks me, "Pastor Carl, can I save eight seats tomorrow for church?"

This would be a cool, reasonable request on its own. What makes it awesome is that Arlene has survived multiple bouts with cancer. In this particular time frame, she was in the middle of chemotherapy. She had very little hair, and what she did have she'd dyed hot pink. Because in her words, "I'm Puerto Rican, and I stay fresh." You learn quickly that when fierce Puerto Rican women tell you things, you just agree quickly.

I said, "Arlene, haven't you been in treatment all week? How have you had time to reach out to people?"

She said, "Well, that's the thing. I was in my hospital bed. I was frustrated with where I was at. And I realized there were people in this place that had it worse than me. So rather than wallow in my own pain, I would try to go lighten another's."

And she became that day a walking revival. Spreading life, spreading hope in the middle of her own storm. Her situation did not change at all. But something had shifted in her spirit.

I want to cultivate that same spirit. *You* need to cultivate that same spirit. Because there is a giant chance that you can maximize the moment that you are in, right now, far more than you ever realized.

own the chapter

Where can you find time to stop and be grateful for all that you have in your life? Rather than chase "more," today is a great day to take inventory of what you have and be thankful for it. Take fewer pictures with your phone and use your actual eyes to make a memory. Put the phone down at dinner and pick up a conversation that may have been cut too short a day ago because less important matters swamped your soul. My favorite moment lately was closing my computer in the middle of something important because it looked like my son was deep in thought. I said, "Roman, what are you thinking about?" He said, "I'm wondering if clouds are bouncy. Like, can you jump on them?" We talked about clouds for an hour. I don't remember what email I didn't finish that night. I'll remember that little voice and our cloud conversation forever. Make the choice to slow down today, at some point, and enjoy what's around you.

Chapter Fourteen

It's Not as Bad as You Think It Is

IF WISDOM HAD A BEST friend, its name would be Perspective. These two weapons, working together in our lives, are an almost unbeatable force. We all know people, have known people, or *are* people who have lacked perspective at one time or another, and it can be a really painful thing. Because so many times in this life we can't change our actual situation. But we can change the way we look at it, and sometimes the difference is life and death. Other times it's the difference between giving up on a job or a person, or shifting our perspective in the situation and getting a better result.

Perspective is that "thing" that keeps you from being "that guy." Have you ever seen somebody who is doing something that they think they are good at, and they are absolutely *not* good at it? Apparently they had not a single soul that gave them perspective that was real. It's "that guy" on *American Idol* who fails miserably, leaves the stage, and is immediately consoled by his mother, who says, "Baby, they don't know. You a star. I raised a star. And we can shine somewhere else." And they leave, and that guy then continues to go through life lacking the simple perspective that, yes, he may be a star, but perhaps not in that particular sky.

This happens to us, for better or for worse. When we lose perspective in our day-to-day, the job we once had and were really grateful for, we now see as a dead end. The project we are working on that we once were passionate about is now a burden. Nothing really changed. Except our perspective.

This happens to single people all the time. They wanted to be married so bad. Their perspective previously was: "Once I get married my problems will decrease, and I'll be so much stronger. Less temptation, less stress. My soulmate is what I need." And then they get married, time and circumstances evolve, and those same previously blissful thinkers start saying, "My problem is that I'm married. If I was single I could do so much more."

Oh, we have all been there. Perspective is so fleeting due to our human nature that is way more prone to defeat than victory, and if you and I do not have somebody who cannot necessarily teach us something new—that's the wisdom department—but remind us what we already know, it's just a matter of time before we make a bad decision based off bad perception.

———————

I remember praying with a friend who was in and out of the NBA for years. He was a quintessential high-flyer, high-volume scorer. Which in the NBA is really valuable—but at the same time expendable, depending on what a team needs at the time. So there are seasons where by sheer luck a guy like this can find himself unemployed and waiting.

So my friend during that time was locked in at church. Front and center. Full of life, full of faith, and I literally remember hearing him pray with me: "God, if you open a door, I will make the most of it. I'll do anything. I'll fill any role. I will take nothing for granted."

God, as He does, answered that prayer. I remember hugging my friend as he was just overjoyed at this opportunity, and for a few months he was an epic teammate. I serve as a chaplain for both NYC professional basketball teams,[1] so I get

———————

[1]My faith is tested more with our beloved Knicks, Lord Jesus help us. At the time of this writing, I'm in pain due to recent Knick decision-making. Actually, come to think of it, that applies to essentially any Knick era, so it's a timeless feeling.

the best view of games, and typically I watch the bench and the body language on the court. It's one of the best and quickest ways to gauge the health of a team. Body language in a basketball context tells no lies.

So, back to my friend: Early in the season, he was waving towels in support. He was the first guy off the bench to congratulate. He was literally "happy to be there." Midway through the season, I noticed his enthusiasm waning. He was slower to cheer. What used to be a quick applause for others was at best a charity clap. One game in particular he was put in the game for what most call "garbage time." (I used to call it "Time to shine." Again, perspective.) He had a breakaway, and as he gathered himself from the free-throw line, he laid it up. For some players, this is no big deal. But if you are a player who is known for dunks, for flash, for fun? This is almost unforgivable.

That was it for me. I found him in the tunnel after the game on his way out, and I asked him what on Earth was going on. He said, "Man, I'm not getting the minutes I want. I don't like my coach. I don't like getting put in at the end of the game." I told him, "Do you remember a few months ago? When you had no job? When you didn't know if you would ever make a roster again? Oh, and also, did you forget that you get paid an ungodly amount of money to play ball? And that you *love* this game?"

To his credit, he said, "You're right. I'm not seeing this

correctly." We prayed together, we rededicated ourselves to renewing our passion, and that guy continued to forge out a pretty incredible career.

I didn't leave him thinking, *Man, I set him straight.* I looked directly in the mirror and asked God to help *me.* Because it happens too often. I want to be the type of person—and I'm surely not alone—who doesn't just visit perspective. I *live* with it. Internally driven perspective is so much more beneficial for us, because it's foundational.

Most people I know have perspective only when something drastic or traumatic happens to them. In NYC after 9/11, almost every church of every creed was packed. Why? Because people for a fleeting moment got perspective that life can literally evaporate before our eyes. That tragedy didn't spare anybody. Homeless people were affected and millionaires were changed forever. Everybody was thinking about what's next. As in, "I need to get my affairs in order or at least have a look at what my spiritual beliefs are."

The problem is that roughly a few months later, churches were back to their typical attendance. Perspective came and went about as fast as the tragedy itself. Rock bottom should be your teacher only one time. In our world, people end up in its classroom every single year.

Is perspective a priority for you? It needs to be. Do you hate your car? At least you have one. Are your legs tired from standing all day at work? At least you have legs. Are you feeling guilty when you leave the house for work because you didn't get enough time with your kids the night before? At least today is a new day, and you can plan better and have the best bedtime story of all time prepared for the next moment that is available. Perspective is present like leaves on the pavement during fall—if it matters to you.

One really practical way to use perspective as a weapon? This little trick I call "ponder before you panic." It's not easy. But when applied, it can save some serious heartache, stress, and knee-jerk-reaction-type decision-making. It definitely requires people you trust, who you train yourself to lean on, because in moments of challenge you can't always trust your own view of things. Your mind can play tricks, and before you know it, what truly wasn't that big a deal becomes just that.

I wouldn't say I'm a hypochondriac, by any means. But I learned the hard way that when it comes to diagnosing my own illness or "potential illness," I am absolutely unqualified. One summer night, I had a minor irritation on my shin that was driving me nuts with the itching. I had been outside, and in the summer I have a "hate-hate" relationship with mosquitoes in that I hate them, and they hate me. So I figured that's what it was. But then I watched some show on TV about mosquito-born illnesses and how they spread. And the longer I watched it, the more my mind began to race. I then compounded my issues by Googling my symptoms.

Let me just state this clearly: Google is great. But if you ever turn to Google for relationship advice or questions about your future, you need Jesus, and you need to come to my church, and we need to talk. Google is a tool, not a guru or a friend.

Anyway: This Google search led me to so many horrific images of shin issues, diseases, and ailments, accompanied by more rabbit trails of exotic shin problems leading to death, that by the time I went to bed, I was sure I had a combination of scurvy, Ebola of the leg, and possibly gangrene.

I went to the doctor first thing the next day, pulled up my pants leg, and said, "Doc, it's bad. I Googled it. I'm in trouble."

You know what he said? You guessed it: "It's not that bad. Not only is it not that bad, it's just a nonissue."

I said, "But sir, I Googled my symptoms, trust me."

And he proceeded to tell me just how many people get themselves into trouble doing just that. He said, "Next time you're not feeling well, how 'bout you go see the doctor? It's not that bad."

I would venture to say at least half of the things that currently keep you up at night, causing extreme anxiety and worry, are not as bad as you might think. And even if they are severe, even if they are truly complex, if you can count on just one person to look over your shoulder in this life and look at the exact same situation and give you some perspective, you will build momentum. You will power through more than you think you can.

Your situation does not have to change. But your spirit can. Your hope can. And sometimes all it takes is one other set of eyes to let you know you're absolutely going to make it to tomorrow.

own the chapter

What does it take for you to not just "get" perspective but keep it? I used to handle some situations in this order: React and then reflect. Typically what would follow would be regret. Because had I known different factors, I would have made different decisions. Now, I'm dedicated to a different pattern that looks like this: reflect, respond, rest. Just writing and reading that brings a different mindset into the equation. Reflect on what you face. Respond to it with intention and confidence. Rest in the aftermath knowing you did all you could do—and move on. Sometimes it's the simple things that help us navigate out of the most seemingly complex situations.

Chapter Fifteen

That Girl Is Poison

IT DOESN'T TAKE MUCH TO derail a destiny. That's one thing that's hard to argue. Although it can take decades to build credibility and solidify a reputation, it only takes a moment to do serious damage. The good news is that much like a car that should get constant maintenance and checkups to avoid the giant blowups, our lives can be built in such a way where a problem that could be deadly is detected very early. In fact, I think we can often avoid allowing the problem to take root in our lives at all. This is called "learning the easy way." Our other two options are "learning the hard way," which is what we do when we take bad decisions and turn them around and somehow get a win out of them, and "learning the tragic way," which is when people make mistakes, pay for those mistakes, never rectify what caused them, and continue to repeat them.

I mentioned a "rock bottom" in the previous chapter for a reason. Not only is it a bad place to learn, it's even worse when people choose to live there, acclimate to there, accept there, and invite others there. I can't count anymore how many times I've been called on as a pastor to help rescue an almost unsalvageable situation only to find that the problem was so minor to begin with. Had people actually gotten help or wisdom anywhere in the process or *before* the process began, it could have been a lot easier.

The truth is that when you see a life implode from the outside—a public fallout, a marriage that ends in disaster—it can look like, "Wow, that happened overnight." It never does. It's a slow erosion of principles, convictions, and standards that were allowed to drift and move, and nothing was done about it. The situation might have exploded in a single day, for sure. But the fuse was lit on that stick of disaster dynamite long before. What's even more frustrating is that so often, it was never something major. But a little bit of "poison" will always end up killing the entire picture. Every time.

Sometimes what is poison in our lives can seem really palatable upon initial presentation. That's why I believe perhaps the most essential way to keep your life pure in the middle of a world that offers poison at every turn might be perspective. I talk about it at length every chance I get, because if you don't have it, you will pay dearly for it. And if you don't employ true friends to give their perspective on *your* perspective? The fight is almost over before it begins.

Enter: the street prophets Bell Biv DeVoe.

———————

Years ago I began preaching a sermon that was inspired by Samson in the Bible, but soundtracked by this legendary hip-hop group. The story and the song are both ultimately about perspective. A quick background on Samson: He was a man who was called by God to live set apart, to live holy, to live powerfully. And powerful he was. Even if you are not a believer in the Bible or its spiritual weight, you should still read this account from the Old Testament found in the book of Judges 16:1–31. It's that good.

Samson couldn't be defeated by other men. He was like an Old Testament mix of Rambo, William Wallace, and Achilles rolled into one man. There is an account where Samson picks up a jawbone of a donkey and destroys his enemies. This guy was special. Sadly, his story includes where he ended his life. He was blind, he was captive, and he was humiliated. Although God honored him at the end of his life with one more heroic feat of supernatural strength, Samson's story to me is sad because he lost. And do you know what took him out and led to his capture? It was not a fierce army. It was not on the battlefield. It was a woman . . . and a nap. A nap!

Samson had a secret that God had tasked him to keep, without exception. But a woman caught his eye, and little by little she wore him down and found him in a vulnerable, exasperated state one day and found out his secret. And that was *it*.

When I read this in real time, I can't help but ask, "Where were his friends?" This guy was a legend in so many ways, but he didn't have one person to say, "Hey, that girl over there? She is bad news. Stop. Let's keep it moving." Instead, he played with poison. I'm sure it didn't start like that or even look like that. But that's the thing about our lives: Most of the things that will take us out, we are not going to see them coming on our own.

The song "Poison" has an iconic beat that will even get white people dancing at a party, and has a simple premise that is basically a warning shot to a friend about a woman he is dating. "That girl is poison!" his friends pled, followed by, "Never trust a big Bible and a smile."[1] I have always loved that song because that's exactly the kind of advice I love to hear and I love to give. Not, "That girl is interesting, but be careful." Not, "I don't know about her, but let's believe for the best." No way, not this crew. Poison.

[1]My remix, lyrically.

When I look at some choices in my life, and I drop my guard for even that half-second and give up on a conviction, make a middle-ground decision even though I have dedicated my life to black-and-white conviction, because I think, "Ah, it will be fine. It's not ideal. It is what it is."—I regret it *every single time*. I want to continue to be a leader, live like a leader, and protect my life like a leader. And there is a cost to that. But I think the alternative cost, of living average, is so much heavier.

I was told by a mentor once, "If you want to live the life of the one-percent influencers, you will have to leave ninety-nine percent of things behind." That is a big call. And it's true. But if that one percent is *great* over good? I'm in.

As you read this, take mental inventory of the things that are percolating through your life, your soul, today. It might not be a girl or a guy or even a relationship, for that matter. That depression that has gone unchecked? Poison. The negative voice that is the loudest voice in your mind? Poison. The habit you have grown to live with and acclimate to and have accepted as normal? Poison. The guilt you still carry from past failures that seem to wrap around your life like a chain that has no end? Poison. You have every right today to make some decisions to purify your life in such a way that you recognize potential poison for what it is: not an option.

When you start looking at your life like that, it's so simple to navigate what you should and shouldn't allow to have influence.

―――――――

I have a list of "primary poisons" that I have seen over the years that are notorious for wrecking people's lives. Fighting for number one on that list? The poison called "failure." If you don't guard against this in your spirit, and constantly clear it out of your heart when you come across it, it's not a matter of if it will affect you—it's *when.* And since failure happens to us all, it shouldn't be as deadly as we allow it to become. When this poison begins to pollute our system, you allow one failure to change the way you see everything. One relationship failure doesn't have to mean all relationships will fail. Just because you made a bad decision and an idea never came to fruition doesn't mean you are not a creative genius with the best still ahead of you. Just because one person let you down doesn't mean all people will let you down. What a shame it is to see somebody never go forward in life because the poison of what has happened has paralyzed them from the promise and future that is yet to come.

I remember inviting somebody to church one time and they gave me a pretty common response: "I'm not coming to church. It's full of hypocrites and I was hurt in a church and I'll never go back." The first thing I always say when given the hypocrite excuse is, "Well, you're right about that. And we have room for one more hypocrite—you—in our church." We all have areas of hypocrisy. It's called being imperfect. So the notion that *that* is a barrier to coming to a church, for instance, is illogical.

But that's what the poison of failure will do. It produces a fear of what can be, because the failure of what has been becomes shackles on your feet. My heroes in life are all people who have overcome failure or a spirit of "finality," which means something is over with no hope of return, by pushing through and keeping their hearts and spirits free. And my heroes are not always historical legends or people who are famous for success. Sometimes they are my current friends who have pushed through unimaginable pain and loss and failure to keep finding the light in this life that can offer so much darkness sometimes.

My friend Levi Lusko, for example, rejected the poison of finality in a situation that I'm not sure I can even fathom. Levi pastors a church in Montana and is one of the kindest and most pleasant people I know. If you met him, you would almost think he must live in a different world, because nobody should be this positive and kind. But that's not true. In fact, he and his wife, Jennie, have been through enough already that

I would say it would be fair if God spared him from facing another challenge the rest of his life. He tells the account of what I will share here briefly in his book *Through the Eyes of a Lion,* which I recommend you get as soon as you can, because hearing this first is life changing.

I heard the news from a friend of mine that I should call Levi because something horrible had happened. When I did, I could barely comprehend what I was told. On December 20, 2012, his gorgeous five-year-old daughter, Lenya, died in his arms from an asthmatic complication that inexplicably led to her not breathing. Levi held his little daughter and gave her CPR until the ambulance arrived, but it was too late. Five days before Christmas, this family was faced with a moment nobody would ever predict and nobody would ever want to deal with.

I have two daughters and I can't remotely imagine life without them. It's a sentiment that most of us dads share equally. So when I heard, I flew to Montana. I had no advice to give, no comfort to offer, but figured the least I could do was be present and offer my love in person. That initial chapter, the aftermath of this tragedy, is difficult to even talk about. Parents are not supposed to bury their children. But they bravely weathered this storm of confusion and complexity, and over time they have stayed on a journey of healing as a family.

If you met the Lusko family today and their four

children—Alivia, Daisy, Clover, and the newest addition, Lennox—I'm not sure you could imagine they went through something so hard. But I know for a fact they made daily decisions to reject the poison of bitterness and finality and hopelessness and chose to extract the often smallest rays of light that could peek through this dark cloud of a chapter. I'll never forget when Levi took me to Lenya's grave two years after she had passed away and showed me what he and his children do each year when they go back and take a moment to remember her life on that day. Montana at this time of the year is blanketed with amazing white snow as far as the eye can see, including gravesites. Those places are sad and morbid on regular days, but it seems even more pronounced when it's cold and snow has covered anything that could make it less nondescript. But you can't miss Lenya's gravesite. Because they take food coloring and draw pictures with it, splash color all over it, just to remember that in the midst of extreme pain, we can still choose to write on top of it whatever we want. They remember her life, not her death. They remember the beauty of who she was and reject the bitterness of not being able to see who she was going to become.

If that was all they ever did, I would respect them immensely, but their drive to find hope doesn't end at bringing color to that specific location. They made the decision as a family to donate vital parts of Lenya's beautiful body to those in need of things that perhaps could be transferred if certain matches were correct. This included her corneas and her heart valves. It just so happened that a man and a woman, ages 53 and 54, had their sight completely restored because of Lenya's eyes. Imagine that: People who were previously blind could now *see*. Even in death, this little angel was literally opening the eyes of the blind. As I write this book, there is this special part of Lenya still functioning on earth and helping other people.

In the midst of the most awful grieving, Levi and Jennie chose to remain sacrificial to the point of donating aspects of their precious daughter, and the outcome was supernatural. So when you ask Levi and Jennie about tough times and tragedy, does the story include pain? Absolutely. They will never "get over" the loss of their daughter, nor should they. But they will continue to get *through* it, carrying her memory day by day. The memory isn't all about loss. It now includes miracles. It now includes others. It now includes *life*. That pain has served a purpose that has changed so many lives already. And it will do that forever because the Lusko family denied the poison of "finality" to take root in that story.

That's the thing about owning hard times. We don't have to "forget." We do have to change what we *remember*. When

Levi talks about his daughter, he won't skip over the part where she left this earth way too soon. He simply won't *stay* there. The story goes on.

It's challenging to me as a dad and friend and fellow pastor on so many levels. To be painfully honest, I simply cannot imagine having the courage that I have seen Levi and Jennie produce daily in this situation. I would not blame them if they lost their faith, were hesitant to love again, and struggled to believe life can still be beautiful. What happened to them is a perfect example of bad things happening to not just good people, but great people. There are no explanations that suffice. There are no well-written clichés that can remotely bring peace on this side of eternity to that level of pain. But he has inspired me to never allow what's wrong in my life to cloud all the things that can still turn out right. He still loves life. He still preaches passionately. He still loves God despite unanswered questions and has decided to use what could be poison as power in his life.

———————

I'm not sure you have ever faced something that seemed so hopeless it has carried into each area of your life. Maybe something has failed, or somebody has failed you, and you find it extremely difficult to believe that you can dream again, love again, and breathe again in the aftermath. If you have? I'm glad you are reading this right now. You can. You will. You have to. Because your story, your legacy, the many people who need to see you move forward will thank you someday for not giving up.

Each time you are faced with looking at something that very well could poison your entire life, remember this: Poison needs permission. We have to give people and situations the right to affect us deeply. We can't avoid bad things, hurtful people, and negative circumstances, but that does not mean we have to allow the permanency of the effect to take root. We often unwittingly have given things permission to live in our lives and hearts that do not deserve that permission. I want to build my life and protect my life in such a way where I am constantly cognizant of the fact that I can choose life-giving positivity over death-producing poison when it comes to what fuels my daily life.

I pray that same revelation opens up your eyes. You are too valuable to not see that poison coming a mile away. Why not begin right now? Own the soundtrack to your own soul. Own the doorway to your own destiny. Make sure what can be is not being sacrificed at the altar of what has already *been*. Your future is too bright to let any other way of thinking even be an option.

own the chapter

If you take a genuine, hard look at what influences you today, the relationships that you hold most dear, are they helping or hurting you? Could it be said that some things that should not even be an option in your life have been given the opportunity to grow? Poison cannot be played with. It can't be reasoned with. It can't be compensated for. So if you truly believe that your life matters and how you feel in private will absolutely affect how you perform and serve and step out in public, maybe it's time to reevaluate how easily you let things get close to your heart. If it's not helping? It's not staying. If it's not making you better? It's not invited to the party. Ever. Replace the poison in your life and you will feel a new sense of power to take ground in so many areas. Own it. If not for you initially, do it for the many who will find hope through you and your story.

Chapter Sixteen

Being Uncool Has Never Been Cooler

I HAVE NEVER BEEN SOMEBODY who has tried to be different just *because*. I think I share or have shared the same desire to please and to be accepted that most people have. There are those people who seem immune from this issue, and I salute you. You're fantastic. But for the rest of us, the desire to "fit in" can be literally the exact thing that keeps us "out." Out of who we are called to be, out of where we need to be, and out of moments we were born to maximize and have influence in.

Granted, I'm not even sure I know what "cool" is right now, and my daughters will far too loudly attest to this. I'm not a spokesman for cool at all. But for whatever reason, over the years, our church has absolutely been hit with the "cool card." As in, our church is cool, and that's why it's effective. Sometimes it's a compliment. Other times it's patronizing and completely void of perspective or context.

What always baffles people is that they simply don't expect to see anybody in church who looks like they do or is outside the box of whatever "church person" they have in their weird little perspective. Furthermore, "cool" doesn't change lives, it doesn't produce longevity, and it doesn't necessarily equate to production. So when people have said to me, "Your church has cool lights and music. That's why it works." I remind them that it's not lights that impact a soul. It's not just cool music that moves somebody to completely change their life. People don't volunteer week in and week out to build a church because it's cool. The cool factor in anything is okay, but that is never what lasts or creates true change.

In fact, in our fast-moving culture, the moment something becomes really cool it's out of style. Now, this doesn't stop people from flocking to things like lemmings to a cliff, and money has been and will be made off exploiting humanity's desperate need to fit in. But anybody who is interested in owning the moments in their lives has to be willing to forsake cool at times and do what is true to *you*. What is best. And often what is best will rage against what is cool.

Think about this: Often the most vital things in our lives are not cool. Being vulnerable is not cool. Getting help is not cool. Being humble is not cool. Being kind, sadly, is not cool. And this might seem relatively obvious, but I know there are many potential great leaders out there in this world who can't break the "cool wall." Because it means stepping out and doing things against the grain. Doing things that nobody is doing or has done. What people fail to realize is that trendsetters, moguls, true pioneers were never really accepted in their time. Only in hindsight do we appreciate things like this.

If you walk out to see a pickup game of basketball, the dominant style still emanates from a crew of legends known as the Fab Five. In short, they were young, brash, mostly African-American[1] players who played really loud, wore impossibly baggy shorts, black shoes, and black socks. Back then? This was not "cool." They did not care, and they had a huge hand in shifting many parts of basketball culture. Our world still needs more of this: people who are secure enough to defy convention and bold enough to take some risks and be different.

I will bet you money that there is something in your heart, something deep in your soul that you believe passionately about but are hesitant to step into because of fear of what other people will think. Here is the first key to this: People actually don't think about you nearly as much as you

---

[1]Shout-out to my guy Rob Pelinka, who gave all white guys hope for rolling with this team. It's under-talked about!

think they do. Most of humanity has their own drama and their own risk-taking apprehensions to deal with. And for those who are left, the ones who may judge you or criticize you, the fact they have the time to do so proves you don't need to care about their opinions anyway. I learned a long time ago: People who do nothing have so much time to talk about others doing much.

When you find people who are enjoying life, making the most of their days, these people did not wake up and think, *Well, who can I impress today?* No way. Those people, the kind of person I endeavor to be? They wake up and say, *I'm going to make a difference today. Somehow, someway. If people like it, they can join me. If people don't, they can watch me. But that will not affect me.*

I remember a day that this vivid reminder was so bright in my face that it convicted my soul. I walked into my normal Tuesday happy place, Chelsea Piers in Manhattan, to play basketball as I usually do. The guys in this gym have become so regular, such a part of my life, it's like its own little world. I love it. But grown men pickup ball is not without the temptation to be "cool." Which totally destroys games and the quality of play in general. Guys try to emulate NBA stars. They take shots they shouldn't. They don't play hard on defense because they fear they can't guard anybody and will fall and end up on some viral video. They spend time actually matching their outfits, as if that matters. And that's just *me*.

Other guys try to be cool as well. It's rare to see anybody honestly "try" or hustle. So I walk in and immediately see a guy doing something out of the ordinary. He was doing old school warm-ups, running back and forth, touching the lines on the court, *sprinting*. Immediately I'm interested. Now, in NYC this alone isn't super weird, because many guys do cocaine before they play, and that is a book in and of itself I shall save. But he didn't stop with the sprinting. He had knee braces, elbow braces, and possibly a back brace—I can't be sure. But the guy was ready to play.

When the game started, he literally clapped the entire time. He dove for loose balls. He chided his teammates for not playing hard enough. His team lost a game, and for about three minutes this guy was inconsolable.

And this is when it got over the top. During the next game, which he wasn't playing in, he stood on the side and cheered for random people. He clapped. He chased down loose balls and ran them back to the court. Please keep in mind, this does not happen. The most verbose pickup basketball exchange outside of terrible church leagues might be: "Yo, pass the ball.

Yo, for real, pass." After that game ended, he went back to wind sprints.

That was it for me. I had to ask him how on Earth he was staying this focused and passionate. Because nobody was getting paid out here. He said this: "Well, I realize I don't look cool. But seven years ago I was shot in the back. I was paralyzed and in a wheelchair for five years. The doctors told me I had no hope to ever walk again. I told God that if by some miracle I was ever able to walk again, I would never take a step for granted. I would never take a game of basketball for granted. I would never take anything for granted. I get it. I look weird. I'm not cool. But I promise you, I have more fun than anybody else out here. I love to play."

I was stunned. I was convicted and I told him, "My man, you are the coolest guy in here." I couldn't stop thinking about it. The rest of the time on the court that day? I took charges. I dove for loose balls. I had *fun*. I left there and looked at my life and thought there was a huge chance that I needed to apply this amazing man's life to my own. Who cares what people think? Life is just too short to be too cool.

And you know what the irony is? The uncool people always ended up leading the way. It's a weird paradox, but also an awesome one. I wonder what you would do if you didn't care quite as much about the opinions of others. I'm glad Steve Jobs was cool with people calling him a nerd. I'm glad Warren Buffett was cool with people saying he didn't dress cool. I'm glad N.W.A didn't care that rapping angry wasn't cool. I'm glad Brian Houston, my pastor, didn't care that it wasn't cool to make sure church services are not three hours long and filled with things nobody cares about. I'm glad Brandon Marshall didn't care that it was uncool to tell people that mental disorders are a real thing and people need to get help like he did.

Almost everybody I admire, at some point, was hit with the "not cool" label. That's why today, if somebody tells me I'm cool, I take it in stride. Because there is a good chance they are referring to a part of me that is absolutely under construction, and just maybe I got lucky and actually was in step with pop culture for a random moment. Those same people will probably tell me I'm not cool somewhere down the road as well. That's why the old adage still rings true: If you live for the praises of others, you will die from their criticisms.

Cheers to the rebirth of the uncool. The road less traveled can be lonely. But there is tons of parking and room to breathe. Own the uncool. It will probably make what you do and what you will do much hotter.

own the chapter

What would you do if you truly didn't care what other people thought about you? How would you live, what would you pursue, and ultimately how much fun would you have? If the overriding reason you don't do something begins with "Because people might think," you need to do some rethinking. Nobody else has to live your life. Nobody else will ultimately have to be accountable for what you did in this life. So it makes no sense for the opinion of others to be the driving force in your life. I think it's safe to say that what makes people attractive is not their "cool factor" but their "unique factor." We are created as originals, so there is no reason to live a single day as a poor copy of somebody else. Be you. It's less work and more fun.

Chapter Seventeen

You Don't Have to Be Good at Everything

I LOVE TO WIN, I shall not lie. In fact, I like winning so much that I will bend a rule or two of a family game if I really feel threatened. Be that Uno, be that Bananagrams, be that Bible memory verses—if I feel my children gaining too much ground, I will creatively flex my "It's my house and I'm the commissioner" label and make sure I get some wins. You might call me a "cheater." To which I would call you "second place."

And therein lies a principle I think is important: We need to strive to win—a lot. There is something inherently wrong with this weird new wave of political correctness that says we can't say somebody won and somebody lost. This is stupid. If my son ever comes home with a trophy for "participating" and his team didn't actually win, I will break that trophy. Trophies, my friends, are for winners. I will go invent a game, have him win, and go get him a giant trophy. My son, though, will never mistake losing for winning. Both are important teachers in life, and we can't pretend that both work hand in hand.

I am by no means anti-winning. I am, though, a huge proponent of trying to encourage others to know it's okay to actually not win at *everything*. To look at some things in life and go, "You know what? That might not be my thing. Or even my primary thing. So I'm going to do what I can, but I'll keep looking and keep focusing on something that I am good at." The need to be number one is why so many people actually never become number one at anything. We start comparing ourselves. We get discouraged or defensive, we try even harder. Which propagates negative moments. And before you know it, you're consumed with things that may not need to hold that much weight in your life.

The best leaders in our culture often have this in common: They are self-aware. They know what they are good at. And they absolutely know what they are *not* good at, and surround themselves with people who are proficient in that particular area. What normally happens? Everybody gets better. And people are generally happier on their journey.

I have counseled people who have their whole lives been

conscious of and worried about what they are not good at. It dominates their lives. They end up losing the ability to see what they are good at, what they were born to do. It's a trap that leads to a really discouraging life. I tell people constantly, "What do you love? What are you passionate about? What do people you know and trust see in you? Pursue that. Somehow, someway, grow in that. There is fulfillment in that alone."

Whatever you do, you don't want to find yourself always trying to prove yourself. Because the only person who loses in that scenario is you. Sometimes it's okay to play in the background, be the B-side of the cassette tape, help somebody else get a bigger win—which often leads to a greater win for all involved.

In basketball terms? It won't kill you to pass.

I have had the privilege of meeting some awesome people, who are *really* good at what they do. As in *the best*. One of my friends you may have heard of is named Kevin Durant. He is gifted—so much so it's annoying to normal people like myself—and he has *worked* to become a master at his craft.

One random really hot day in July, after he had worked out and I had watched and learned and pretended that I too worked hard at stuff like he did, he wanted to play two-on-two to wrap up the workout. There were only three guys in the gym, so obviously I put my hand up and said, "Of course I'll play." To put this in proper context, three out of the four playing were professional basketball players. In late July, post-season, almost every pro basketball player I know doesn't want to be in a gym or even think about basketball. So no games are "games." This is work, it matters, it's business, and typically it should be left to professionals.

But I have a professional basketball mentality. Meaning what I think about myself is most likely not in tune with re-ality, basketball-wise. But whatever. Don't judge me. I am a survivor, and of course I was all in to play in this game.

I ended up on Kevin's team, and I actually did survive. Did it help that Kevin carried the load? Sure it did. But this was a team effort. The game was to 21, and Kevin had 18. The other guys also had 18, and we had the ball. Kevin passed me the ball, and I promise you, I was open and I had room to shoot. So for the first time all game, I let that thing fly.

And I missed. And they got the rebound, quickly kicked it out and scored, and we lost. You read that correctly: I am the guy who lost a two-on-two game with Kevin Durant! Literally, I had one job in this scenario, and it wasn't to shoot.

Afterward he said, "Bro, why didn't you pass it back?"

I told him, "Bro, I was open and I'm a shooter. This is what I do."

He said, "That's fine, but I'm a better shooter." He shook his head in disgust and walked off. We walked out of the gym, and we haven't spoken of that game ever, ever, ever again. This game cost me twenty minutes of silent treatment from perhaps the greatest scorer the world has ever known.[1]

But if you look at your life—and absolutely when I look at mine—are there times you force things for the wrong reasons? Are you fixated on things that in the long run really won't hold much weight with our higher calling and what really matters? I don't think God put us on this Earth to be good at everything. But I am certain He created each one of us so uniquely that we are here to do *something* that is extraordinary and will impact others in a real way. Maybe knowing what we can't do is almost as powerful as knowing what we can do.

I've heard it said that the space between what we say and what we do is who we really are. I like that. There is peace in the middle of that. After you read this today, take some time to reflect on what you love, what you're good at, and who you aspire to be good to. Don't get stuck thinking and dwelling

---

[1] I asked Kevin if he was comfortable with my sharing this story in the book. He said, "Of course. I'm still mad about it. I think about it sometimes." Keep in mind, he won the NBA Finals MVP a week earlier. The guy loves winning, people.

and confined by what hasn't happened just yet. This world needs the best out of you almost as much as *you* need the best out of you.

own the chapter

I once heard it said that "a jack of all trades is a master of none." I've known so many people who are trying to be good at so many different things that nothing ever sticks. Projects never get finished, gym memberships never get used, promises go unfulfilled. That's no way to live. I think there is power and peace to be found in focusing on something you love and pouring your life into it. Pouring your passion into it. Find something new, by all means, to expand your experiential bank account. But if you have found something that fuels your soul? Take advantage of it. Become proficient at it. I think it will end up leading you into more, but it won't be at the expense of what you have right now.

Chapter Eighteen

I Demand Something Different

I'VE MET PEOPLE WHO SAY they want to change. They are articulate, they are genuine, and sometimes they even convince me. The problem is that the *idea* of change is much different from the *reality* of change. Desperately wanting a family is such an amazing idea. When you actually have your own family, your own kids, and all that comes with it? Please believe me: There are times when you want to ship your little children straight to Siberia and never speak of them again.

The idea of changing your life and how you value it is inspiring. I don't know anybody who wakes up and says, "I want to impact not a single soul today. I hope I am a complete non-factor and that this day is over quickly." I think inherently we all want to leave a legacy. We all want to experience more than the daily grind of this life. We just don't know how.

One of my biggest irritations being a pastor of a church is when preachers preach fantastically inspiring messages with absolutely zero practical applications. I call those "handles" in a sermon. Meaning if I give you a beautiful, expensive car and you get in it and there is no steering wheel? Good luck with that. This happens in church all the time. People will stand up and shout down and *amen* a preacher, and then you ask them, "What are you excited about?" And they will say, "I'm not sure. But it's exciting!"

Motivation is fantastic. Inspiration is awesome. But it actually can't produce anything meaningful in our lives. It's supposed to be in addition to a true desire to change that is immediately followed by decisions that leave no other options.

One of my best friends is very inspiring and hilarious and spontaneous. He's the kind of guy who says out of nowhere, "Hey! Let's go make grape jelly. Who doesn't love grape jelly? Matter of fact, grape jelly is under-talked about, and we can make money if we do it the right way! We can manufacture our own jars too!" Before you know it, you are all in. Roughly two hours later, after you have spent money on supplies, read up on the jelly trade, and are awaiting further instructions from your fearless, inspirational leader, you find out he left to go vacuum his house and can't even recall the conversation about jelly.[1]

Inspiration is not the problem. Things in our lives change when we make decisions that shut the door on any other possible exit. Don't talk to me about eating healthy with doughnuts on your counter. Don't ask me about finding relationships that matter when you have that new dating app on your phone that has produced exactly zero meaningful connections, but they hoodwinked you by giving you access to photos of people you will never know, thinking you will know them, but you can't stop swiping and liking and DM sliding no matter how fruitless it may be.

I always say that if somebody is serious, their decisions will give them away. This is one of the reasons I am a follower of Jesus. I have friends who are Buddhists. One of my best friends here in NYC is a devout Muslim. I to this day study all I can about what other people believe so I can better understand people I love who adhere to a different faith system in life. And I can say this without hesitation: Jesus offered what nobody else, spiritually speaking, has ever even claimed to offer. Jesus offered salvation and forgiveness and hope and peace. Which are inspirational

[1]Love you, Joe Termini!

things, yes. But He would follow with a *how*. With crazy things like, "If you want to live (inspiration), you must die to yourself and pick up your cross daily (application)."

I've heard a few spiritual gurus give inspirational talks, but when it gets down to it, they use words and phrases like "enlightenment" and "your truth" and "put no borders on it, growth happens." Those are all code words for "I actually don't know. And you can't quantify or clearly define enlightenment. But most people don't know that, so I'll build on that." Listen, enlightenment is fine. It's even cute. You know what I want? I want direction. I want instruction. I want application. And I would bet that you do too.

I personally will not allow an inspirational quote I love to go without putting directly next to it a personal application handle that I actually *don't* love. So on my wall, I might have: *BE THE CHANGE YOU WANT TO SEE IN THE WORLD.* Yay! Who doesn't love that? I can put that on a shirt, go to Coachella, and sell that T-shirt. But I can't allow something meaningful to not include a challenge, to make sure I'm not fooling myself. So next to my *BE THE CHANGE YOU WANT TO SEE* I write under it: *Speak with kindness to your wife, and pick up your shoes at the door like she has asked.* Nobody is buying that T-shirt. But guess what? If I make that little decision? It will lead to another. And another. And now my inspiration has fueled my actual life. Not just my dream world.

I think it begins with demanding change from yourself. And you can start with your spiritual appetite. If you are going to change, if I am going to change what I see going on outside of me, it's going to start with what I am doing to get better, to change my soul, at the core of the inside of me. Technically, what we desire, our appetites in life, should grow as we grow.

To a degree, this does happen. I look at what I want at age thirty-eight, in contrast to what I wanted at, say, twenty-two. And it's really funny how what you desire has drastically changed. When I was twenty-two, I loved Escalades and big SUVs and I thought rims that spin were incredible.[2] But now, at thirty-eight? I don't care about SUVs. I don't care if my rims spin or gleam or floss. In fact, I don't even need to have rims on my tires. You know what I'm interested in? Those little cars that you plug into the wall. How far can I get on that charge? How much will I save in gas money?

What you desire *should* change. I no longer go to amusement parks with giant roller coasters with my kids and think, *This is going to be so fun! Let's do it!* I think, *Is this safe? Have people died on this before? Is the guy operating the machine HIGH? Because*

---

[2] If you are "young and hip" and find it funny that I liked spinning rims, you probably have a fidget spinner. So I don't want to hear about it.

he looks high, and I'm not getting on a ride operated by this guy who has a hemp necklace and keeps giggling about the way the trees are blowing. No way. I desire safety way more than I desire thirty seconds of roller coaster elation.

Have you checked what you desire lately? What you have an appetite for? If you don't desire change, if you don't desire to make a difference, you need to demand it in your own life and follow through with some decisions that will bolster your new demand. Not only will it affect you, but it will begin to impact others. What seems like a small decision that follows a big demand of yourself could lead to somebody else getting a breakthrough in their life.

––––––––––

I remember praying one day that God would help me live with peace. I desire peace in a major way, but I don't want to live a life free of pressure. Because that also means a life free of impact. I just don't want the pressure I deal with to crush me.

I hate anxiety and I hate unrest, and apparently our culture does as well. There are more types of anti-anxiety medications on the market and in circulation today than ever before. Because I am a Christian, I have a huge advantage in the war against anxiety, and that is my prayer life. I don't hold any beads. I don't have to go to a priest and sit in a confessional and confess to another human all my sins. None of that. Because of Jesus and who I believe He is, I can pray, at any time, and know that it's going to help me.

My problem is not that idea, it's the follow through. So that day as I prayed that God would help me cultivate peace in my own life, I left that moment of prayer and decided that I would live by this phrase: "Before I panic, I will pray." I demanded of myself that I would make this change. This meant that any time, any place I felt pressure or stress or fear or whatever, I would take a moment and I would pray: remind my soul who God is and what He has saved me from. And then I would go about whatever it was that I was doing.

You know what started to happen? After the prayer, the panic or fear or stress had a much weaker hold on me. One decision to stop and pray.

One pressure-packed day in particular, a friend and I were rolling through Williamsburg, Brooklyn, and this day seemed like the Baskin-Robbins ice cream day: Instead of thirty-one flavors, it felt like thirty-one failures. I found out a friend of mine had relapsed. I found out our church wasn't able to use a particular venue that we needed for the upcoming weekend. And—though not as important but it still totally mattered—my favorite NBA gunner, J. R. Smith, was injured, which meant the Knicks game that night would be less interesting.

We have all had these days, where it seems like if it's gotten bad, at least you have worse to look forward to. And as we drove, and as I went through the list of frustrations, I remembered my decision—that I desired peace in my life, and I was gonna do what I had to do to get it.

So I asked my friend to pull over on this Brooklyn side street, which was attached to a little park that overlooks the East River and is equal parts beautiful and Brooklyn. *Beautiful*, meaning you can see the entire city from there, and it's spectacular and eerily peaceful in a place it should not be. *Brooklyn*, meaning you had to step over a syringe or two and absolutely watch your back, as this place was known for transactions of all sorts of items.

And on this day the park was a Godsend. I stepped out of the car, walked for a moment, prayed, and I didn't magically feel better. I did, however, feel like at least I had control over my spirit. My situation? Not so much. But it wasn't going to rob me of my joy that day.

And as I walked back to my car, I heard somebody yell, "Hey! Pastor Carl!" I had thought this park was empty, but I was wrong. This man came running over, and he was not a small man. So immediately I wished I had tied my shoes up. But I stood there. And he approached me with tears in his eyes. And he said, "I go to your church. We have never met, and it's crazy I would see you here. Today has been the hardest day of my life. I lost my mom yesterday. I am struggling to deal with it. I came to this park to pray. I have felt alone, I have felt discouraged, and I prayed today and asked God that He would send me anything that would encourage me. And here you are."

When I tell you I couldn't care less what two grown men crying and hugging and praying together in a park looked like, I mean it. When I got back in my car, I couldn't stop thinking about how awesome that moment was. You know what I wasn't consumed with? The things that, yes, are genuinely pressure packed and real and difficult to deal with—but not worth destroying my mind or my peace. You know what helped me that day? Not my inspirational thought about how "prayer changes things." Not some cool hashtag that says #theuniverseislisteningwhatareyousayingtoit. It was a small decision I made that backed up a desire I had. That ended up helping me in a small way that day. But the residual and collateral effect of my decision to bolster a desire to change in my own heart led me to actually be the answer to somebody else's prayer that day. It wasn't luck.

It happens all the time. Life is funny like that. If you look at pizza? You will desire it. If you look at photos of vacations all day? You will want to go on vacation. If you look at change, if you look at people, if you look at our world and desire to make an impact? You will prove it by putting this book down[3] and writing down not what you dream about but what you demand of yourself. And for each demand, write down a decision that comes with it.

You never know where this small step will take you, but I have a feeling it's going to be fulfilling.

own the chapter

When we see the word "demand," sometimes the connotation is negative. For instance, when people want something more, they bring a "list of demands." I propose this idea isn't wrong as long as you bring that list to yourself. Sometimes we demand and expect things from others that we don't demand of ourselves. If I demand that my wife, Laura, speaks to me with kindness, yet my own self-dialogue and internal vocabulary is negative and discouraged, I am fighting a losing battle. What do you demand for your own life? What are your nonnegotiables? If you stick to those, you will attract a new type of person in your relational world and won't need constant motivation from others because you take care of that. You will always be the loudest, most listened-to preacher in your own life. So make sure you are "preaching the truth" to yourself, every day.

[3]Just for a second.

Chapter Nineteen

I'm Listening But I Don't Hear You

THE CONCEPT OF PURPOSE BEING a dynamic driving force in our lives is not new. We all want purpose, we all need purpose, and we have all been designed for a purpose. What separates people, though, from thriving in it or failing in it sometimes comes down to how we handle those around us as we try to navigate what we feel passionately about.

There is a quote that has floated around for a long time— I actually used it as my high-school senior quote: "If you don't stand for something, you will fall for anything." I credited the quote to Tupac, but I'm not sure he said it first. It just looked cooler than crediting it to Aristotle. Regardless of who said it, it still holds a lot of weight in my life, and I will tell anybody who will listen to me here in NYC: You better know exactly what you believe in and what you are passionate about, because if you don't, this city and this culture will be happy to tell you.

This is exactly why fashion changes weekly, why morality in general is on an epic downhill slide, and why more people don't do amazing legendary things. Anything that takes time, anything of value, anything remotely different typically does not come with applause, doesn't come with a lot of support. And since we crave those things so much, often we abandon things we are purposeful and passionate about because people sway us one way or another. We have to learn ever increasingly how to stand strong in what we believe, so we don't get swayed when things get challenging.

I heard a preacher say one time, "Be careful you don't spend your whole life buying things you don't need, with money that you don't have, to impress people you don't even like anyway." That is funny, and it's true. Think about how many decisions you have made over the last few years that were solely based on the approval of others, on what they would or would not think. I have made a few. And almost always I regret it.

Anything significant I have ever done is normally a decision that the majority would question. And even if I do have the courage to actually do it, once you are in it, you tend to listen to other people telling you how to function in that particular lane.

I'm talking about Twitter.

Social media has produced a way for people who would not naturally have a platform to have one with a microphone. When I was growing up, I couldn't tweet Michael Jordan and tell him that I didn't approve of his faraway jumper and that he needed to get Luc Longley more involved. But I found it amazing this year, as I watched the NBA playoffs, how many "expert" opinions were being directed at the players. One genius told LeBron James, "You need to stop driving into the lane and shoot more deep threes like Steph Curry. You suck, LeBron." Forget the fact that LeBron James was created on planet Cyborg, is actually related to Ivan Drago from *Rocky IV*, and is an impossible force of havoc driving to the lane. This guy on Twitter? *He* knows better. And he let LeBron know.

We can laugh him off. But what we can't laugh at is just how many people are handcuffed in their own purpose because they allow the voices of far too many to discourage them.

When Laura and I decided to pastor a church in NYC, I think I absolutely cared what people thought. But at the same time, we absolutely did not. We knew our goal. We knew not everybody would like it, but far more would like it. But I still got a shock when I realized just how hard it is to "please people."

When you run a church, you prepare for criticism. You prepare for people to sometimes unfairly talk about you, say all kinds of things. And you learn how to deal with it. Comes with the territory. I thought we would perhaps make waves for the standard stuff. Drug dealers mad because we severely hurt their bottom line due to people no longer being addicts. Angry boyfriends sending me letters of hate because the girlfriends they were cheating on and treating like garbage came to church, realized their worth, and left them on the curb. What I didn't expect was people who would criticize us for actually doing good.

To give this context: If you're not familiar with the "Christian church world," it, like all other circles of life, is riddled with insecurity and terrible thinking. It should be the opposite, but such is life. In fact, it may be worse, because Christians like to make their pettiness sound spiritual. "I'm only saying this because I love you." Rather than cheer for somebody who is winning, sometimes church people find it easier to try to poke holes in what they see. Because it's far easier to tear somebody down than to look in the mirror and be challenged and convicted to grow in your own life. And this is why you have to know what success means, what winning means, what your purpose is to you—so you don't end up allowing others to manipulate what should be joyful to you into something that becomes joyless. My purpose actually protects me from poisonous persuasion.

Our church exists to see people radically change because of what God can do in their lives. Whatever it takes to get somebody in that position, to hear about Jesus, to hear about grace, to hear about redemption, we are going to do it. That means we don't care what you look like. We don't care if you have your "church clothes." I don't care if you smell like a one-man reggae concert because you smoked weed in your car for two hours prior to church. Our passion is to open up the doors of the "church" and welcome people home.

Now you may read that and say, "That's great. Seems logical." Well, often the most illogical voice in your life or in your world can be the loudest. It's a warning to take note of. So over the years, there have been times when we have had to break the mold, to make sure we stay true to our purpose.

One time in particular, we had a break between services. At this time we had seven services every Sunday and met at

Irving Plaza, a very cool venue in NYC that usually has rock shows. In fact, we would sometimes find out that people came to church because they hopped in the line thinking it was a concert. Whatever it takes, we don't care.

But after one of the services, some friends and I took a walk a few blocks to get ten minutes of air before the next one began. We sat down on a curb. It was hot, and we were tired. When I say tired, I mean exhausted. Early on at Hillsong NYC, I was preaching six, sometimes seven services on a Sunday—each about forty-five minutes to an hour long. I wouldn't describe my preaching style as "sharing a thought." There is very little sharing. There is a whole lot of passion, and each service is different, and the message comes out in different ways. At the end of every Sunday, Laura would tell me I looked like I was in a daze, and the Monday after would be hard for me.

Sometimes the things you would least expect to refresh you when you are that tired end up doing exactly that. As I got up to head back, I saw a man in the corner—as you often do in NYC if you have not immunized yourself against seeing actual hurting people—and he was slumped over holding a beer can. It was obvious it had been a very long time since he had had a shower, a good meal, or even an interaction with a human. He had a hat on that read "Vietnam Vet." That always increases my urgency even more because my grandfather was a proud Marine who was wounded in battle fighting for our country. Veterans matter to me.

So I walked up to him, and we talked. I gave him what money I had, and I did what I almost always do: I invited him to church.

He looked at me with kind, tired eyes and said, "Son, no church would let me in. I smell. I am a drunk. And to be honest, I gotta have a beer in hand to even sit still for thirty minutes. And this beer can is empty."

I said, "Sir, I happen to know the guy who runs this particular church. I can tell you for a fact that you would be welcome. And you know what: If it helps, I'll buy you a new beer. You can hold it, drink it, pour it out on the floor of the church—whatever you need to do. How's that for a deal?"

He was in.

I wish you could have seen his face when he walked in and was greeted with hugs. Was greeted with dignity. I stood next to him for the first part of the service. Then when the time came for me to preach, I told him, "I'll be right back."

If I had a camera on his face when he put two and two together that I was the actual preacher, it would be worth money. He smiled ear to ear. He leaned in and listened to the whole message. At one point I grabbed my water to sip and said what I always do as I drink it: "Cheers to anybody new in church." My friend held up his beer in the front row and said, "Cheers back at you. Thanks for the beer, Pastor!" It was awesome.

After church, we prayed together. We talked. We got him involved in some things that could help him slowly piece his life back together. It was one of those nights that you don't forget—and of course you have to post it on Instagram. So I did. This was back a few years ago when I didn't have quite as many people watching our every move. But I thought, *Surely this is a story that will encourage everybody. I'm gonna post it.*

The next day I opened up Instagram and looked at my comments. Yes, some normal, rational people had left some reasonable, expected comments, along the lines of: "Wow." "This is great!" "Thank you!" You know, the minimum compassionate human reaction to a story such as this.

But there were many people absolutely up in arms that a man had a beer. In church! Or that a man had a hat on. In church! Or that I bought a man a beer to come to church. Things like: "Carl, you sold out. You have gone too far." "Hillsong Church has gone off the deep end. What a joke. No respect for the house of God." And much worse.

I would love to say it didn't bother me. After all, we prepare for this kind of thing. We knew we would ruffle some feathers. But people were seriously taking shots at the way we chose to love this homeless man who has nothing? I didn't handle it well. I'm far from perfect, especially with my low tolerance for Twitter warriors or the troll bandits on social media. I went back at them. And so did others who love us and possess, you know, common sense.

I looked at the posts the following day—the comment wars, the vitriol in the back-and-forth—and in that moment I had a moment. I thought, *Isn't it interesting that the actual purpose of why we came to this city has not wavered. In fact, it's thriving. What is affecting me are the random comments from people I don't know, who don't know us, and will never know this fight we are in.* I reminded myself of who we are. What we are called to do. And I made a fresh decision to be resolute in my purpose and never be swayed by the voices that have a lot of opinion about the fight but no blood equity.

Criticism is always a win-win situation. Because when you are rooted in your purpose and secure in your calling, you realize that if what people have said about you is true, you have to change. *Win.* If what people have said about you is false, you have to be more confident in what you're doing because you know the right people are mad. *Win.*

I will never be the type of person so arrogant or falsely confident in what I do that I dismiss all uncomfortable feedback and write it off. In fact, I will be the opposite. I will listen to people. But I will hear only a few. Like Wesley Snipes told Woody Harrelson in *White Men Can't Jump,* when Billy Hoyle was trying to say he was a Jimi Hendrix fan: "You can't hear Jimi. You may listen, but white people can't *hear* Jimi."

You need to own your purpose, own your calling, to the point where you can handle whatever is said. Where you don't believe the hate about you, because it's probably false. You don't believe the hype about you, because it's probably false too. You live right there in the middle. That's where the truth most likely is. If you have a dream in your heart, a passion in your spirit? Run with it. Stand by it. Build it.

By the way, Instagram ended up creating a feature where you can disable comments under the photo. Sometimes it's better to just post and not look back. Perhaps there are some voices and some comments and some opinions about you from people that you need to remove permanently from your soul.[1] If you don't, negative opinions and seeds of doubt can take root where they don't belong. They can grow when they never should have been planted in the first place.

As a leader, I always try to teach others to make sure you

---

[1] I find it suspicious that most social media trolls have blocked accounts. It reveals much about them. Don't give too much time to those who criticize your public life from behind their own private little walls.

investigate before you capitulate. Meaning, make sure you had a really good reason to change and bend and compromise on something. If somebody wants to change something and I ask them why and they say, "Well, they think I should," my first response is always, "Who is 'they'?" Normally what follows is, "Well, everybody." And I say, "Cool. Name them. Name everybody." Typically, they can name about two people and that's it. I love to point out how amazing it is that two people almost spoke for everybody and got you to make big sweeping changes. Be careful of what words and ideas you let sit in your soul.

I like when you can delete comments on Instagram and then double down by blocking the person that sent the comment. Instagram sends you a message that says, "This person will no longer be able to find you on Instagram and see what you post. You can choose to unblock them at any time." This was hilarious to me when I found it. Over the years, I have stopped checking Instagram comments because it's so ridiculous how many people think they have the right to cast long-range judgments on matters they literally know nothing about. I used to try to answer people out of a genuine hope that understanding could be found, but rarely did that actually happen. In fact, the moment you answer it's like the person thinks *I matter! What I said mattered and I was right, I knew it!* And then they keep writing.

On the other hand, if you don't respond people will say things like, "No response? See, I'm right. Silence means everything." I would see these and think, *Okay, let me get this straight. If I answer your opinion or comment, I'm guilty because why else would I defend myself? If I don't answer, I'm also guilty by not answering. So either way, the random troll wins?* How silly is this logic? So now, I look for the longest, most robust comments I can find, the ones where somebody uses your platform as their platform because they don't have one, and I delete it and block them. Not only do I not have to accept it or read it, nobody else on my feed has to either.

The life implications of this are absolutely endless. When it comes to who we are, what we believe, just because somebody said it doesn't make it true. You have the right to block, delete, and move on in life. Choose to listen to the voices that you love, that you trust, and the rest should never even land on your radar.

In the course of one week not long ago, I was called "an amazing pastor who helps so many people" and "a cancer to the city of New York that needs to be removed." In the same week. I went home that Friday night and just for fun, as I contemplated the insanity that is public opinion, said to Laura, "Hey, babe. Who am I?"

She said, "Ummmm, you are Carl, my husband?"

I said, "Cool. Thought so."

I went to my kids' rooms, and I said to each one, "Who am I?"

They all said, "Dad, you are *Dad*, duh."

I walked downstairs, called my mom, and said, "Hey, Mom, I love you. Who am I?"

She said, "You are my son. You are my sweet, sweet boy."[2]

It remains true in this life that it's never *what* people say about you that matters. It's always *who* says what about you that matters. If you get the right "who," it won't matter when "they" try to discourage you from doing what you feel called to do.

I live for an audience of one: the God Who saved my life. So it's really easy to know whether I'm right or whether I'm wrong. Maybe it's time for you to ask: Who are you living for? One thing I do know: It can't be for the approval of many. You're called to a greater purpose than that.

---

[2]She has said that to me so many times it's not even awkward to type.

own the chapter

We need to fortify our ability to "put on the headphones" when necessary in this life. One of the cutest things my son still does is talking extremely and awkwardly loud on planes, when he has his earphones on. I'm talking level 10, when level 2 is all that is required. It's like he doesn't realize other people are talking, or it may be quiet, and he doesn't remotely know the volume climate of the area. Although we are five inches away he will yell, "DAD! CAN I HAVE MORE PRINGLES?" I have to tap him and whisper, "Son, you are yelling. Take those off when you talk to me. Yes, you can have Pringles." In one sense, though, I pray he lives like that as he grows up. Sometimes it's better not to listen to all the noise. Sometimes it's better to not hear the noise of the crowd around you, so you can focus on what you feel called to focus on. Especially if you're smart enough to put people around you who will tap your shoulder once in awhile to let you know, you need to hear something important. What are you listening to today? Is it hopeful? Is it life-giving? As you change your surroundings, keep some headphones close by. There will probably be some noise you need to block out.

Chapter Twenty

The Problem Called People

I THINK IT'S BEST THAT you sit down and read this in a quiet space. I have to begin with an audacious claim that I believe is continually tested but will always be true. You ready? People are awesome. They are fantastic. They are life giving. They are far more than meets the eye. They are unique, they are completely complex and absolutely complicated and beautiful. And on top of all that? We need them. Here is the problem, though: People are not perfect. Often people are reckless with their imperfection, and if we don't properly plan for this problem, we start to distance ourselves from the one thing that is not going away in our lifetime: people. So we don't have a lot of options when it comes to how to navigate this life with some people we would never, if it were up to us, be around in the first place. You will love some, you will be tempted to hate some, but every single "somebody" matters.

When we think about people, maybe it's helpful to first realize the obvious. It's likely that the people you hate come to mind much quicker than the people you love. The next thought is related, painful, and true: We are a lot more like the people we hate than we realize. Sure, our issues might be more palatable and our flaws might even be more understandable, but we all have areas of our lives that somebody in this world absolutely can take issue with. Realizing we are all under construction makes it more bearable when you are forced to pursue positive thinking toward others when they may not deserve it. If you are silly enough to think you are a one-human show—that "I ain't never needed nobody!"—please call your mother, thank her, then slap yourself. Not a single person on Earth has existed without help from another.

The baseline of thinking about how good people really are is important, because our world seems hell-bent on tearing people apart. Whether it is your skin color, your political party, the social class you have been assigned to, the amount of money you do or do not have—the division is like a swarm of mosquitoes. Unless you completely step on it and destroy it, it will ruin your life at some point. You will get bitter. You will get defensive. You will eventually develop a bias and even a prejudice toward those you do not yet know, due to previous experience, previous teaching, or assumed future experience. Stated simply and purely: We can't kill people.

So we might as well learn how to own our relationships so we can look around and be thankful that we get to do this crazy thing called life, with people who we love. And it is possible. If that window isn't open, we are all in trouble. And for many, it is not open. I fight people on their negative, definitive mindsets all the time—from loving people again to even attending church. As if some bad moments now get to dictate everything that is to happen in the future.

―――――――――

I asked a guy to come to church one time, and he said, "Hell no. I don't do church." I said, "Why?" He said, "I grew up in a terrible church. Terrible people. Hated it. Never again." To which I said, "No problem, I get that. But please make sure you are consistent in your logic. If you have ever eaten at a bad restaurant, you can never eat out again. If you have ever been in a car accident, you must never, ever use a car again. If you go to a doctor and he wasn't exactly right and that bugged you, you may never, ever look to modern medicine again."

It's stupid logic for church, and it's even worse for people. I have met people who are so defensive you can't remotely challenge them on anything, because they grew up around mean, attacking people. I know others who are so wounded from being burned by somebody, they simply never trust again. You know what the irony is? You become the exact thing you hate. Somebody was attacking you, so you by default become defensive. Now anybody who even comes in your direction, you attack! It's a painful twist to something that probably wasn't even your fault in the first place. But we can't allow our sick culture of shallow relationships to seep into our adult, growing lives.

Why is it the older you get, too often the less people you know? By and large we are not getting better at this, we are getting worse. I, for one, am not having it. One of my 43 million life goals is to have better relationships when I'm seventy than I did at thirty. Better in no way means "more"; it means that I never stop trying to make the lives around me better. In that scenario, I have no choice but to grow. I promise you, I will pull this off.

And what's funny is that it's actually easier than you think. Because there is such a void of friendship in this world, if you just do the baseline minimum that is required for human decency, you will look like a saint and a legend. I'm serious. If you hold the door open for people in New York? They are shocked.[1] Of course, I learned this lesson vividly about the minimum requirements for changing the world on a basketball court.

I have always loved shoes. Especially basketball shoes. I'm not one of those odd people who buy basketball shoes and either keep them in the box or, like, wear them to dinner. I actually play basketball in my basketball shoes. But somebody once told me that if you really love something, try giving it away. I wish it was something I could "unhear," but it stuck. So the next time I went to play ball, after we were done, I took my shoes off—please note they were brand-new, otherwise that is super weird—and gave them to a guy I just met because I thought he was a nice guy. He was kind, very funny, and from what I could tell didn't have a whole lot of extra money to be buying new basketball shoes with any frequency.

The guy takes my shoes, looks at me, and goes, "What are you doing?"

I said, "Clearly, I am giving you my shoes."

He said, "Why?"

---

[1] Except for one time. I held the door and this woman said, "I don't need your help, man. Just because I am a woman doesn't mean you need to hold the door." I said, "I'm not holding the door because you're a woman, I'm holding the door because I'm from Virginia. Get over it."

I said, "Because I think you'll like them. It looks like you appreciate shoes, and it is what it is."

He sat silent for a bit. I left to go to my car, and he chased me down and said, "Look, bro, I appreciate it. That's one of the nicest things anybody has ever done for me."

I told him, "My friend, you need better friends."

I'm still friends with that guy to this day. He didn't "need" my shoes. It wasn't charity. It was just something that should happen.

My point is that my personal world is simply as friendly as I want it to be. You don't have to give shoes out, but you absolutely need to leave your house every day thinking, *I wonder how many great people I'm going to meet today.*

As crazy as it sounds, it's gonna happen. Intention is a funny thing, and so is default. There are a lot of people I know who complain about their life and the people in it, not realizing that you actually don't have to accept what you see. You can change your settings. Your default relational setting is on "me." If you make this one switch to "others" and see everything through that lens, you will enjoy the fruit of that in your life.

Have you ever heard anybody disparaging somebody behind their back, saying, "I can't stand that person. All he does is think of others. All he does is encourage, and show up on time, and do what he said he was going to do. In fact, I'm going to avoid him today in case he pulls another 'random act of kindness' on me or something. Avoid them at all costs. They are too thoughtful." Doesn't happen.

People are *still* amazing, despite what you may have legitimately experienced in the past. We have to turn the relational pages in our lives. Maybe it begins with how we see people in the first place.

own the chapter

Solid relational wisdom to build on when it comes to having good people around you: Be the kind of friend you want to have. Sounds simple, but many people miss it. Rather than focus on what your friends don't do for you, and how much more you wish they would do, it's a fun switch to just try to embody all the values you want reciprocated in this life. What you will find is that you begin to attract who you are. If you want encouraging friends? Be an encourager. If you want people to stop showing up late to events you plan? Be early to theirs. If you hate it when people only contact you when they want something? Don't be that person. Relationships are a reflection. If you don't like what you see in people, the best place to start changing things is in your mirror.

Chapter Twenty-One

I Am in the People Business

IT'S ONE THING TO RESIGN yourself to the fact that people are unavoidable and we have to learn to "deal with them." Hopefully, the previous chapter opened up at least an avenue to a new way of thinking about humanity, because I believe the more we endeavor to love and serve people, the more fruitful our lives become in general. I'm sure you have seen interviews with people who seem impossibly happy, from corporate CEOs who don't just make money but also make people's lives better to people with extreme disabilities who somehow seem to light up every room they enter. I've often found that these people, upon further study, don't just love people because of what those people can do for them—they just love people. End of story. Almost as if the return they get on their love investment will never compare to the joy of the investment in the first place.

I watched a documentary about a man who started a small business that grew and became world-renowned. The success of the actual business was inspiring on its own. But what really struck me was the joy the employees had when talking about this legendary CEO. Almost every one said they would work there forever, because they knew the "guy way up top" cared about them. They, in turn, cared about him. The business was a by-product of that. This was not one of those weird, cultish interviews about a boss who forced his employees to say nice things. This was real. When they finally let the man speak for himself, his simple answer was, "I am in the people business. People are my business. I happen to sell other stuff too."

Wow. It's little wonder that this man stands out like he does. I don't know many people—I don't know many *pastors*—who think like that. Normally, we settle for loving people with conditions: if they perform, if they pay us back, if they help us produce the bottom line we want. But this guy? He's onto something. I think it should be said of all of us, no matter what we do, that we are in the people business. Because we are. The alternative is to live a life in which we almost churn through relationships like shoes that go in and out of style. We wear them out and discard when needed.

There are many examples available in history—or maybe even in your own personal experience—of bosses or CEOs who have an aspect of success but can't figure out why they can't get or keep good people. I know people who are wealthy but they are bankrupt relationally and have to spend their money on themselves because nobody likes them enough to be around them. This is what happens when you buy the lie that "life is about you"—that people are about you, that everything revolves around you and ultimately comes back to you.

I believe inherently the opposite. Life is about others. My money is about others. My faith is about others. My relationships should be about others. And in a divine twist, you know what happens to my life when I stick to this? My life gets better. I feel fulfilled. Caring about others is not to the detriment of yourself necessarily. In fact, it just might be the most beneficial thing you could ever do.

Sometimes in my life, people have seen me in a particular relationship with a person who is well known and they don't understand the context or the journey. Laura and I have always had this motto with people: "If God puts you in our path, we will love you." We do not care if you are broke and smelly, or rich and haughty. We don't care if nobody knows you or everybody knows you. What people *do* is not important to us. Who people *are* is.

If you live by that like we always have, you find yourself with a U-Haul truck full of stories, experiences, relationships, and impacting moments. Because the road of genuine relationships is wide open, there isn't a lot of traffic on it, and it continually winds upward.

I was with a young pastor one day who said to me, "I want to pastor NBA players someday. I see you do it. I want to do it. I'm on the lookout."

I said, "On the lookout for who?"

He said, "NBA players. Athletes. People of influence."

I stopped the conversation right there, picked up the fork from the table, and stabbed him in the eye. Or at least that's what I felt like doing. And then I realized there was a moment here to shed some light.

I spent the next hour or so telling this truly awesome guy that everybody has influence. Some are more pronounced, but we don't actually get to pick and choose who we love in this life. We are called to love everybody. We are called to affirm the dignity in everybody. The way we love people will absolutely change. You can't love a deaf person the way you love a person who has hearing. You have to learn sign language. It works that way with everybody. Yes, people who have a lot of money and worldwide fame need to be loved and encouraged in a way that makes sense to them. And it's going to look different in almost each and every relationship. Works the same way with a drug addict, a single mom, a college senior. The thing that can never change is our respect and love.

I told this guy that rather than being on the lookout for NBA guys, go to the local high-school game. Go support people who you *do* know. That may perhaps lead to more things down the road. But right there lies the key: The goal is not to love people and build relationships so that they can produce more. That's called networking, and most networkers are universally loathed. The goal? The prize? It's the actual people.

If we learn to love that, and value people for who they are, right now, I have no doubt that, yes, it may perhaps make you more efficient relationally and you just might be somebody who reaches a wide range of people. The difference is that you can take it or leave it. You don't need it to fulfill you or make you feel more secure. You already had that in the people you were blessed to know.

I haven't always known NBA players. Over the years, stories have come out and photos have been posted, and I've had the blessing to meet guys who play my favorite game professionally. I've never once brought up a single name unless it's been asked or approved by that name, or to defend that particular name. One minor irritant of the media spotlight is that you can't always control what they write.[1] One reporter said, "Lentz dropped the name of five or six athletes he personally mentored." In reality, the reporter asked whether I knew these individuals, to which I replied, "Yes, and I won't comment further." So in fact that reporter was the name-dropper. I digress, yet feel great. Reporter, you know who you are.

These relationships intrigue people, and I get that. But let me shed some light on how things like that really come about. I don't think I knew any NBA athletes or "famous people" of any kind before I moved to New York. Proximity has a lot to do with passion by the way. Often we have no passion for something simply because we are so far from it. Schools in the inner city that don't have proper textbooks for their students rarely end up on the news, and you don't see many fundraisers for books. You know who cares about them? The parents of the kids in the inner city. Because it's literally affecting their homes. Speaking about racial issues, for instance, is often a complete nontopic in some churches because they have zero diversity whatsoever. Why talk about how race affects people in church if the issue will never come up? Conversely, if you

---

[1]Feels good to write a book for that reason alone, matter of fact.

lead a church that has multiple ethnicities represented, you better believe it's a topic.

Proximity leads to passion.

So when we moved to New York City, our new location and position put us in proximity to new problems, new people, and new passion. We began to get a passion for the people of this city, which included the nameless, the forgotten, the homeless we now saw right on our street. It also included the well-known. They, too, were on the street we lived on. The New York City culture literally spans that whole spectrum of humanity. We didn't seek famous people or homeless people. We were after a city that included both. We went to New York because we wanted to go to a place that was a cultural touch point in America. Period.

One of our first weeks in New York, I met a man named Rex. He was immediately memorable because when I preached, I always knew he was there because he would yell "Amen!" so loudly and so genuinely that if I didn't feel confidently in what I just said, I did now. I got to meet him after a service one day and found out about his life. He had been preaching in homeless shelters, on the streets, and mainly in prisons for a long, long time. He told me he loved our church, he was committed for life. And he's one of those guys who, when he says it, you know he means it. We began a relationship. We met on the streets, and he would introduce me to people I would never have gotten to meet otherwise. Rex would walk me down some streets and introduce me to locals and lifelong New Yorkers—from shop owners to guys who cook hot dogs on the street.

One Sunday in particular, Rex was doing his "Amen central" thing, I was preaching, and there was nothing out of the ordinary. One of my staff members came up and said, "There was a new couple who came to our church today. They loved it but mentioned that Rex was pretty loud, and they wondered if that always happened. They prefer a quieter atmosphere for church. Would you like me to mention anything to Rex?"

I laughed and I said, "Don't tell Rex a thing. Rex is good. I'll ask him to be sensitive to the moment maybe. But honestly, Rex preaches in prisons. He feeds the homeless. He is actually out on these streets and has dirty hands to prove it. Let Rex be."

I don't think the other couple came back. To be honest, in a church like ours, if that kind of thing irritates you, you're in trouble anyway. New Yorkers can be funny, though. As if every single thing in life needs to be the exact thing they want. Our church actually rages against that.

But Rex did come back. Every week. One Sunday he said to me, "Carl, I'm leaving church today to go pray for the New York Knicks at their chapel. Do you want to come?" I said yes. Not because I liked the Knicks—I was actually raised a

Chicago Bulls fan—but because I liked Rex and wanted to see how he was gonna do this. And I had never been to a chapel, had no idea what to expect, and it would be really interesting.

NBA chapels, I would come to find out, are a complex operation on a few levels. It's cool that the NBA lets it happen, and I have met some of the most amazing men who have been serving a particular team for a very long time. Almost all do so on a volunteer basis. They receive zero compensation from the team, and are people who do what they do simply because they want to help players grow in their faith in the midst of a uniquely challenging profession. That said, there are practical barriers that keep guys out of chapels that are very fixable. Simple things like when the chapel is actually held, time-wise. It's usually sixty minutes before the game. If you had to pick the worst time to speak to people about anything of depth and spiritual significance, this would be the time you would pick. The game is looming, guys are trying to stay loose, the pressure is palatable. And even more weird: Both teams are in there together. You haven't felt an awkwardness like that extreme team animosity mixed with chapel "I must make peace for twelve minutes" obligation. But that's almost always what happens. Guys put aside their differences and find unity in shared belief. Sometimes the mood can be somber and heavy. Other times the chapels can be uplifting and fun, depending on the chaplain. It's a lot like church in that regard. One NBA player would not come to chapel, and he said, "Carl, I tried going to chapel early in my career, but I always left feeling worse and more confused. So that's a no-go for me." It's not a perfect construct by any means, and it's a challenge for any speaker to be effective, considering the variables at work in this atmosphere.

Yet this did not affect Rex. He preached loud, like there were twelve hundred people in the room rather than twelve. And it was powerful. Afterward, Rex grabbed the broken wrist of a certain seven-footer way too quickly and said, "Let me pray for this wrist!" And I gently pulled his hand away and said, "Rex, let's just pray and not touch his hand at all." It was hilarious.

On the way out of chapel, in the deep dungeon that is Madison Square Garden, I bumped into a legend named Allan Houston. Not only was he the assistant general manager of the Knicks, he was a Christian. We became friends. Allan introduced me to one of his friends, a guy named Chris Bernard. He ran player development for the Knicks, and we became friends. (Lifelong brothers, matter of fact—I officiated at his wedding not long ago.) Somebody asked if I could come to a few Knicks practices, one thing led to another, and I ended up helping out with random things, like chapel or whatever was needed to support these guys.

That November, I was standing on the court as I do as teams were warming up, and a guy with connections to both teams approached me and said that he loved Hillsong music, that he was praying for our church, and that a few of the players were genuinely pursuing a real relationship with God. He asked if I would pray for them. I said I would absolutely, and I asked where and who they were.

He said, "I didn't mean *now*. I just meant when you think of them." We both laughed, and I said, "I'm thinking of them now."

He said, "Well, I will tell them. Do you mind waiting in the tunnel after the game?" Quick note: For every game I have sat courtside—which is amazing, and I will never, ever, ever turn down free tickets no matter how many people question how I got them—I have spent a hundred games in those tunnels. It might be a two-minute hug and a prayer and "I'll holler at you later," but trust me, it's as unglamorous as it gets.

After this game, I did wait around, and this guy came out and said, "So the guys who want to say hi are Kevin and Russ. They will be out soon." A few minutes later, the greatest pure scorer the world has ever known sauntered out. We hugged, talked, and I gave him a Bible. We have been friends ever since. This is easy, because Kevin Durant is so easy to love and is as thoughtful and kind as you could ever imagine.[2] Russell

---

[2]He owes me a championship ring, because he is a man of his word. But I'll keep that between us and this book.

Westbrook came out later, looking impossibly cool. And as te-nacious and hellacious and any other *-acious* you can come up with for how he plays, you won't meet a more humble, soft-spoken, yet still pretty terrifying human being. We prayed, we talked, we exchanged details, and Russell and I will be friends for life.

I am so happy I met them. I love them. I'm proud to be their friend and some small part on a team of encouragers in their lives. But what I never forget is how a guy like me ended up being in the path of guys like them. I didn't wake up hoping to meet transcendent NBA stars. I did wake up praying that I would honor every person I met, value every relationship I have regardless of what it might produce. And sure enough my life is filled with people you may not know, who helped me be in a position to help some people you *do* know. People like Rex and many others in my life, who helped open small doors or windows that I otherwise may never have seen or walked through.

A few months later, I found myself in an absolutely freezing Oklahoma City swimming pool in the back of a sprawling mansion. Kevin had made such a deep commitment to follow Jesus that he wanted to renew his passion and reaffirm his call-ing by getting baptized.

If you are not familiar with this, baptism is not something you do as a baby, when somebody sprinkles you with water and then you grow up and somebody says, "Oh yeah, you're baptized." That's fine if that is your tradition. But you also had zero control over that. We believe baptism is essential to our faith, a public confession of a private decision to let the world know Who you follow. It's symbolic of your old life, your old sin, getting completely covered by the grace of God and buried in that water. And when you come up again? It represents a new day.

To be a part of this in anybody's life is an honor. So to be there with Kevin was special. And afterward, I thought about Rex. Surely he was somewhere, baptizing somebody who nobody knows and having the time of his life. Just like I was.

It's possible in this life to look over the "nobodys" in your search to be around the "somebodys" and find yourself searching for meaning along the way because you look around and see "nobody" who you actually know. And the whole time? It could have been "anybody" who you were looking for. You just didn't see it, because you had your eyes on the wrong thing.

———————

Could there be somebody in your life you have overlooked? Could there be somebody you have undervalued because you were standing on them rather than standing with them? People

are the greatest thing God ever created. Own every relationship like it matters. Because it does.

own the chapter

Do the people in your life feel valued, loved, and appreciated?
I know in my own life that if I feel valued and appreciated, my
effort and my passion increase dramatically. Conversely, if I feel
like somebody is tolerating me because of what they think I
can do for them, rather than actually liking me simply for who I
am, I have to really dig deep just to do the minimum required.
Because value matters. Being respected matters. Maybe in our
world, the key to getting "ahead" is to slow down and get to
know the people in your life. It doesn't take much to let people know they matter. I try to take 20 minutes every day, and
thank people who consistently produce joy and peace and
confidence in my life. Maybe you don't have 20. But if you start
thanking the one or two that are faithful, don't be surprised
when you have got to make more time to thank people. Because more good people will find their way into your life. Value
leaves a trail that is easy to find.

Chapter Twenty-Two

Maybe We Are Not So Different After All

WHEN YOU DO WHAT I do for a living, which basically comes down to listening intently, praying passionately, and doing your best to shepherd and guide and correct wisely, you learn a thing or two about the human condition. You learn patterns. You learn tendencies, and you see commonalities in people despite how radically different they are.

One thing that is common is the fact that everybody tends to think that whatever they have going on has happened only to them. Their struggle, their pain, their dependency, you name it—they are the first to deal with it. And this works well with our other natural propensity: to isolate ourselves when we struggle or when we feel like we are dealing with something

— 217 —

people don't understand. And as I have stated previously, isolation breeds insanity. There is a reason that our prison system equates our highest level of human captivity with the words "solitary confinement." Meaning we are going to strip you of every conceivable way you could feel connected to anybody else. From what I have heard, it's horrific, it's painful, and I'm not sure how we still allow this in our society.

Nonetheless, you don't have to be in prison to be living in solitary confinement. Maybe you are reading this now, and you think: *I don't know if I'm going to make it through this. One thing after another.* Or: *If anybody knew what I was dealing with, they would run.* Oh sure, on the outside? You may very well appear to have it all together. But I've been around enough people who "have it all" on the outside to know that what you see is not always what you get. We are good at keeping secrets about ourselves. Which is fine, until you hear something that is very, very true. Like, "You are only as sick as your secret." Ouch. Possibly double *ouch*, depending on how much you might be holding inside.

But here is the encouraging thing: We humans? We are not as different as you think. Especially when talking about where we hurt, what we deal with, how we cope. It's actually shocking when you delve into this. Sure, some of the symptoms we deal with can be very different. But when you trace something back to the very root of it, you start realizing, for instance: "Wow, I have multiple, unfulfilling sexual relationships not because I am some sort of freak. But because I have never known true worth. That's the *real* issue." Or, "Maybe I self-sabotage my life when things are going well not because I am a failure but because I fear success after watching my mentor throw it all away when they had it all." Reasons are not excuses. They can simply help us find answers to real problems. To aid and abet this toxic turn in our culture, we live in the Twitter-Instagram-show-your-best-hide-the-rest world, where there is no way the image of you is anything close to the real you.

Sometimes it's comforting to know that we are not alone in this life. That there is nothing, with God's help, we cannot overcome. Nothing. I don't even have to know just how bad it is for you right now. The fact that you're breathing means there is hope. I have learned this time and time again, through meeting people and having friendships that remind me if I can just be honest in this life, I can keep moving forward. And the things that keep us apart so often in life? They can end up being what link us in really special ways.

For instance, often people will disqualify themselves without anybody else knowing. They may cheer for others, they may outwardly seem okay, but the real story is that, due to something they are dealing with, they have put limits on themselves.

I used to pray, "God, make me extraordinary. Make me a leader of leaders. Help me be special and stand out from the crowd." One day I realized that, yes, God can truly change my life. But I'm always going to be a guy from Virginia, who's about 6'2" with a really short attention span, a guy who loves passionately and at times allows that passion to get him into trouble, a guy who makes mistakes. All the time. So if in fact God did answer my prayer and made me "extra special," who on Earth could I reach? Who could I relate to? Maybe my state of "average but under construction" can be really useful. I don't know anybody who is extraordinary or perfect, but I know *plenty* of people just like me. I started to get encouraged just thinking about it. On top of that, my knowledge of Jesus was increasing: my revelation of what "His grace" means, which at its core is literally things you did not earn, ask for, or deserve, yet God gives them to you anyway. And I began to think differently.

Over the years, I had heard so many speakers—preachers in particular—who tell you these ridiculous stories and feats of amazement intended to encourage. But they are so far removed from your average life that you think, *Really? I can't live like that.* And you feel worse.

You know the stories I'm talking about. Where a guy will get up and say, "Yes, I am a man of prayer. I talk to God. He uses me. In fact, I got on a plane the other day. There was turbulence. The pilot got sick. And I went up and flew the plane. God tends to put me in the right place at the right time. After all, I am a man of God. When I left the cockpit, the passengers cheered and said, 'You didn't have a copilot and still did it!' I told them, 'Ohhhhhhhhh, yes I did. Jesus is my copilot.'"

Mic drops, crowd cheers . . . and regular people like you and me with real-life issues leave saying, "I'll never win. I'm having trouble and feeling depressed." Or "I'm having trouble not chain smoking." Or "I'm a single mom and I can't deal with my children." Or "I'm pretty sure I cheated on my taxes again." Slowly but surely, we disengage.

When I found out that God could use me in my weakness? That my pain and my struggle and literally showing people my worst might encourage somebody else to dig deep in their life for the best? I was elated. If it's about failures? I have millions. I have material for days. My at-best average life? It resonates with people. Who am I trying to kid by acting like I don't deal with the same stuff as everybody else? My life continually reflects, I pray, what God can do with "average." Our church, no matter what you have read or heard, is a collection of average trophies that God uses as He will.

We have a saying that brings hope to everybody who hears it: *"Every scar has a story."* You might not like the scar. You may even believe that if you could do it over again, you would avoid the experience that caused the scar in the first place. But the fact remains that you have scars. I have scars. The question is: How will you use them? If you can tell a story that saves somebody else from having that same pain? Then roll up your sleeves and tell somebody about what you have been through. It might be exactly what they need to hear to get through something in their own life.

One thing we cannot do when it comes to overcoming weakness that holds us back is to look at what we struggle with in isolation. That's why talking about pain in a constructive way can be so helpful. You quickly find out that, yes, your issue may be difficult, but when other eyes are on it and some new perspective is added, you realize it's not as bad as you had previously thought. And on top of that, people can simply relate to "disqualification" in general—the feeling like you are on the outside looking in. I know personally that when I became a "weaker preacher"—meaning I intentionally set out to talk about what I'm bad at as well as what I'm good at, where I have lost in addition to where I have won—I became a better preacher. When people give me feedback or encouraging stories about something that I said that helped them, more often than not they resonated with something I struggled with and fought through or am currently fighting through. Struggle doesn't have to separate us. It can be the major thing that connects us as people.

This topic leads me to Tyson Chandler and Justin Bieber: two people who, if we are counting wins and relatable lives and occupations, I have absolutely zero in common with.

Tyson I would consider one of my best friends on Earth. For years, we have shared our lives, our pain, our struggles, our families, and our cars.[1] He and his wife, Kim, are very special people. The Bible talks about those who have a "gift of hospitality," and the two of them own the market on this. They are faithful and loyal and have that ability to make everybody feel like family, even if they are not. They inspire me in so many ways, including what it means to look out and care for those you love. They were a part of our church for years while Tyson played center for the Knicks, and although we have on the surface nothing in common, our pain, our shared love for our families, our passion to be more than two guys taking up space on this Earth have always brought us together. I've learned from him, laughed with him, cried on him, and was also with him when he wanted to get baptized again, to renew his faith and his passion. (This will be relevant later on, trust me.)

I'll never forget the day in Calabasas that I called Judah Smith and asked him to come help me out in this most special

---

[1]Well, the cars, that's more me driving Tyson's.

of occasions. Judah is a dynamic human being, and no matter what the setting, he makes it better. I knew his easy laughter and poignant words in these moments would be important.[2] I called and said, "Judah, we are gonna baptize Tyson. It's gonna be tricky 'cause he is a legit 7'3". So we gotta do this in deeper water in the pool. Be on your toes." Sure enough, as we leaned Tyson back, Judah got caught up in the riptide of a small pool and a large human and too-deep water and Tyson basically crushed Judah. We thought we lost him underwater for a minute there. And when we (meaning I) brought Tyson back up, Judah had unwittingly been baptized again too.

That was a special day for me, because it was a perfect culmination for how Tyson and I met. We had connected on our struggles, our real-life ups and downs, and to now find ourselves in a pool, praying. Moments after doing something symbolic of your weakness, being overmatched by God's grace: That's what baptism really is. God's grace *covers us* when we accept His forgiveness, and this visual—a person being pushed backward before they are lifted up again—is not by happenstance. That's exactly how true growth happens and true change begins. God's

---

[2]Funny story about Judah. Years back you would hear a lot of preachers on podcasts, but videos were not as big a thing just yet. Judah came to speak at our church one time and afterward one of my friends goes, "I just can't believe he's white! He's so good, I thought he was a brother! Matter of fact, I'ma go tell him he's officially black. He's that good."

mercy and grace and power aren't "sprinkled" like dust on us, according to how good or bad we have been. That's why we don't just put a foot or a toe in. Baptism is explosive. When you come out of that water and feel fresh air on your cold face, you don't forget it. It covers you. All of you. Weakness? Yes. Grace? Even more. All of us in that pool had "been there." Little else was relative. Tyson, who is from Compton and was drafted straight outta high school (see what I did there?), and won multiple gold medals, a Defensive Player of the Year award, and an NBA championship was a successful businessman. And Carl, who had no achievements even remotely close to those. But in that moment and since? We have been as close as you can be. Trusted confidants. Who would have thought that a bridge called weakness could cover so much ground, so quickly?

Later that month, post-baptism, I watched Tyson get a tattoo—or, more specifically, a line through a tattoo. One of his first tattoos was an exact replica of the one Allen Iverson made famous. It was a bloody dagger with the words *ONLY THE STRONG* inscribed around it. That day, Tyson got a black line right through the word *STRONG*. He said, "I don't believe that anymore, but I don't want to cover the whole thing up. I want people to see the word *STRONG* crossed out. So I can tell them that only the truly strong can admit when they feel weak. And when we are at our weakest, God can do the most in our lives."

He didn't know it at the time, but he was quoting the

Apostle Paul who said, "Therefore I will boast all the more gladly in my weakness. . . . For when I am weak, then I am strong." It's one thing if I say that, because I'm a guy who isn't particularly strong anyway. But coming from a guy who looks like he was drawn in a Disney cartoon room as an invincible basketball villain with 2 percent body fat, a guy with a Compton scowl that is perpetual unless you see him with family and loved ones, a guy who gets technical fouls for yelling "Gimmmmme that shot!" (but uses a much better word than *shot*)— coming from him it becomes even more real. I can't relate to his strength. But when it comes to understanding weakness? Even I stand eye-to-eye with Tyson Chandler.

Just to "double down" on how much I believe you can help way more people than you think you can just by realizing you have way more to offer than you think you do, let me tell you for a moment how Tyson Chandler and Justin Bieber will be forever linked in the coolest way possible.

My relationship with Justin has been covered a fair amount in the press. It's important to note that almost 98.9 percent of what you read about him is utterly false. One time we were at dinner at my house, playing Uno with my kids as a matter of fact—with Justin conveniently changing Uno rules, because even Uno bows to the current king of pop—when a breaking news alert hit my phone: *Justin Bieber destroys NYC club with reckless party.* Cool story. Problem was, the night in question he was at my table. Again. Eating all my food and encouraging my children to make fun of my age.

No doubt, Justin has made his fair share of mistakes that have been legit. But perhaps we can all collectively shudder at the thought of all our mistakes being covered by a worldwide press. And those mistakes simply speak to who he is and who I have always said he is: a man who loves Jesus, who tries to get better day by day, who is not perfect and never claimed to be. He's kind. He's extremely thoughtful and caring, and he's a genius who is frustratingly good at almost everything. I recently saw him learn a song, in Spanish, in one day. And record it. And do it so well people didn't realize he doesn't speak Spanish! And again, I'll belabor this because it's important: If you became world famous at roughly thirteen and were thrown into a life of music, fame, money, good and bad people, and the ability to influence millions of people around the world, how do you think *you* would do? In that context? His life is a miracle. The fact he is so kind is a miracle. Hanging out with him for any amount of time, you can see exactly why so many stars turn to drugs, go crazy, or, even worse, want to disappear forever. He has fought for normalcy in a rabid culture that does not want to give it to people like him. So I'm proud of him, and I have learned a lot from him. We have had our fair share of rash judgments thrown at us, false stories written about us, and situations looked at without context yet still speculated upon ad nauseam simply due to our relationship with Justin. But all that comes with the territory, and we counted that cost a long time ago and made peace with it.

I met Justin through Judah—he of the previously mentioned "baptism by accident" and world-renowned preaching gift. He called me one day and said, "I'm working with this young guy, Justin Bieber. His mom used to play my preaching to him as a kid. He's a really awesome young man. I think you can help me support him." So over the years Judah and I have had the blessing of being in Justin's life, in many different chapters. But what always stuck out to both of us is that probably the most famous young person on earth, with all that comes with that, needs exactly what Judah and I need. Love, support, feedback, a listening ear, pushback at times, and vulnerability.

People always ask, "What's it like talking about life and Jesus with Justin *Bieber*?" (And they say his name in that weird way.) I always say the same thing: "Matter of fact, he's just like you. And just like me." We can't connect on a money level: He has more. We can't connect on a fame level: He's known all over the world, while sometimes I'm not sure if my children even remember I'm their dad. You know what Justin and Judah and I all share? What it's like to be lonely. What it's like to want to grow in areas that are hard to talk about. What it's like to be disappointed. What it's like to make mistakes that affect people we love. I think the only way I would *not* be able to be a real friend to Justin or Judah is if I acted like I had no issues, if I always wore my "brave New York face."

There was a day when perhaps I would have taken offense at being known as "the guy who cries a lot," which is how some people refer to me. But I'm cool with it now. I'm certain that if I wasn't like I am—flawed and fearful quite frequently—I would not end up in situations that are very close to being unbelievable.

One cold January night in NYC, Judah, Justin, and I had a really deep and real conversation about faith, about choices, and about surrender. Justin told us, as he always does, about the ups and downs of his calling and said, "I want to get baptized." We were both like, "Awesome. Great choice. We will hook that up. July sounds good, right?" Justin said, "No, I mean like right now. I want to start fresh tonight."

Even in the best of circumstances, there are not very many "optimal baptism spots" open to the public. But make it two o'clock on a January morning in NYC and add Justin, paparazzi, legions of insane Bieber fans who somehow—like angels or demons, depending on how you look at it—seem to know his every single move, following him everywhere he goes: This, my friends, is a challenge of epic proportions.

But we were up for it.

We tried a few different places. First a hotel with a pool, but that was shut. Then an apartment complex that would have been viable, but the security guy took out his phone and began filming Justin and calling other employees to come "look at Justin Bieber." So that didn't work, either. At about three o'clock, after exhausting the Brooklyn options and most of Manhattan, we even thought about using the East River. But I figured baptism was supposed to be about "new life," so it would be a shame to not make it out of that river alive post-baptism due to whatever it is that floats in there.

And then I said, "Guys, I have a random idea."

I called somebody who I knew lived in a fancy building with a pool.

I dialed up Tyson Chandler.

Never mind he had just played the Miami Heat, it was the most intense time of a tumultuous Knicks season, and Tyson was probably, you know, tired. This was urgent. He picked up his phone, and I explained the challenge.

"Bro, I got my guy JB with me. He wants to get baptized tonight, and we are out of options. Can you possibly get us in your pool?" And this is what Tyson said: "Nah, that pool is locked up, and they won't open that till morning. Tell you what. My bathtub is custom-made. I bet that would work. Y'all come through." I said, "Are you sure? I'm sorry it's so late and this so random." Tyson said, "Nah, I've been there. I know that feeling that he has right now. When God puts that on your heart, you gotta do it. Come through, and that's that."

We walked in—not to a dark apartment and a sleepy owner begrudgingly opening their door, but to Kim Chandler, who somehow looked gorgeous. And she had food ready. Because, please believe me, if the Chandlers have you over, you will eat, and Kim will tell you exactly where to eat, and how to eat. You will feel like you are family even if you are not, because these Chandler people know how to love anybody who crosses their path. Kim said, "Glad you are here. Love you all. If you don't take your shoes off, I will cut each of you with the quickness. You too, Justin." I call her "the POTUS" for a reason.

We walked into the coolest bathroom I have ever seen and filled up what was in truth a bathtub but one made for a literal giant. It easily fit Judah, Justin, and myself for this purpose. We prayed together. We took a moment to just be still and think about how far God had carried us all. And we baptized Justin, in Tyson Chandler's bathtub in NYC at about four in the morning. So for record-keeping purposes, you have a pastor from Seattle, a pastor from Virginia, a mega pop icon from Canada, an all-world basketball player from Compton, all in a room together. It sounds like the beginning of a joke. Except it's real.

We all shared the feeling of needing to start over.

To be forgiven. To be loved without conditions.

To be looked at through grace, not judgment.

We need more of this in our world. We need more people to be just as clear about the confusion they face as they are about the catapult-like moments that take them to new heights and accomplishments. Because at the end of the day, if the whole purpose of this life is to make others better, I'll use my loss so you can get a win. I think we can safely call that a "win-win."

own the chapter

Your brokenness can be a bridge to somebody else's wholeness. It's counter to our culture, to choose to be vulnerable enough to even acknowledge our weakness, let alone share about it so others can learn from it. Yet there is so much power and freedom in it. It's one thing to share about your success stories. It's an even better thing to encourage people who may be on a similar journey and could use the encouragement that comes with knowing they are not alone in some common struggles. Your losses in life will resonate with far more people than your wins ever will. So who can you encourage with your story? Who can you lift up by letting your guard down? If it could make the difference between somebody choosing to live another day or give a risk again, it's worth it every time.

Chapter Twenty-Three

It Ain't the Dealer's Fault

THE FIRST TIME I RENTED a car, I drove away after getting all the details and paying the cost, and I thought about how funny renting something is. You don't have to own it; you can, to a degree, do whatever you want to it that isn't "permanent"; and when you bring it back to the rental place, you can just leave. It's incredible.

I remember off-roading in a Chevy Malibu in some random town with a friend I shall not name,[1] and I remember eating in the car, tossing my trash in the car, leaving the beach and, rather than kick the sand off outside the car, doing so

---

[1] Joe Termini.

inside the car. Why? Because it was not mine. Now you might be thinking, *This guy is a terrible person for doing this.* That's fine. But I think *you* are a terrible person for pretending to act like you have not done the same thing. So we are even.

But it's very true that ownership produces value. When you own something, it reflects you, it affects you, and it *projects* you. So suddenly things that didn't matter? They matter. I know people who take really good care of things that others may think have very little value because they own it. A little piece of ownership is far better than many pieces of "rentership" anyway.

Sometimes people's lives can be headed in a disastrous direction, sometimes overtly and other times covertly, and you know that it's just going to continue because they won't take any ownership at all. It's always somebody else's issue. Always. If they were late? It was the traffic. If they didn't get a promotion? The boss hates them. If they keep getting hurt in relationships? Always the other person. I remember one time a young girl, after yet another heartbreak, said, "How do all the bad guys seem to find me?" I told her, "Girl, I think it may just be the other way around."

If you are always at the scene of the accident, you may need to go invest in a mirror and look into it very intently. Sometimes the most usual suspects are hanging out in plain sight. And they look eerily similar to you. Why is this? Because of course it's just easier to blame somebody else.

I used to watch *Jerry Springer* all the time. Jerry, if you are reading this, cheers to you. Well done. You looked at our culture, you assessed it properly, and thought: *Most people are just stupid and bored. Therefore I will feed them this and they will love it.* You nailed it.

My favorite episodes were when Jerry would put up a guy with his "girlfriend" only to reveal the man had, in fact, another girlfriend. In a predictable yet never-get-old succession of events, these women, upon hearing these utterly shocking and out-of-nowhere bombshells of truth, would attack each other. Hair would fly, fists would fly, typically censors would fly due to excessive clothes lost during battle. It was always a spectacle to see.

But my favorite part was the guy. The actual guy who did the cheating and the lying and the manipulating? He would normally go unscathed. And even hold a mini-tryout—each woman given equal time to prove who loved him more. I would always think, *If these girls would team up and go punch the guy in the face, and go find themselves their own decent guy, this would be so much better.*

But that would also be too real. We can all laugh at a talk show dumpster fire of humanity at its worst. But I have—and you know you have—attacked the wrong thing at times because we don't want to take ownership of the one thing we can actually change. Ourselves. Our mentalities. What we will and won't accept in our lives. Maybe the problem is not everybody else. Maybe the "world" isn't out to get us. Maybe we have spent too much time stopping our own momentum, not realizing we are the actual blockage in the flow.

———————

I learned this lesson the hard way. When you're a pastor, sometimes you can want to help people so much that you try to do the work for them. Even assist them in blaming other things because you don't want to force them to confront the real issue.

I had a horrible run-in with a drug dealer one time in lower Manhattan. A friend of mine was abusing heavy drugs, and I had just left his house with one of my guys who was equally upset that we seemed to be making no headway with our friend. It was almost like we wanted him to be free more than *he* wanted to get free.

When we left his house, we ran into a person who we knew for sure was his dealer.[2] We waited for him to come out of our friend's apartment later than night, because I honestly felt like that if I could just tell this dealer that he could go poison anybody else on this street but leave this one client, my friend, alone, I would greatly appreciate it. I think I had

———

[2]In NYC you learn this stuff quick, and I'll leave it there.

unwittingly started to shift blame to this dealer. And surely he was a factor. But the truth is, it is literally a "free-trade drug market" in New York. Nobody *has* to buy.

Predictably, this dealer didn't appreciate my approach. But I didn't appreciate his, either, and it was clear that this impromptu meeting was not going to end well. I think the fact that by this time of the night I had five friends with me, and the fact he had none with him, helped this meeting end quicker than it would have.

A few days later, I got a call from this same dealer. He told me that he'd found out who I was and that he was actually looking forward to meeting me. Not to thank me but to "teach me a lesson." He had heard, I guess, that my church was hurting his bottom line in general. I told him he had heard right, and I would love to meet him. (I have a history of reacting first, thinking second—and it's not a strength.)

So I had a meeting lined up. But before we met, I called a friend of mine who is also in this same line of work, only in New Jersey. We met playing basketball and became fast friends despite the fact that we were two very different types of "dealers," if you will. But I called him to let him know what had happened, and I also wanted to know if this was going to make a difference. I said, "If I convince this guy to stop, one way or another, will this matter in the long run? Is this guy a serious player?" My friend said, "Oh Carl, you should leave that one alone. That guy is with a crew that is based in Eastern Europe. You want zero part of that crew. But if you got a problem, we can handle that. Just say the word." I was like, *Noooooooooo*. I didn't say I want it "handled." I told him I just wanted to do whatever I could to help my friend get clean.

And my guy from Jersey gave me some advice that landed. Sure, I have heard it before. But there is something about current need that plays into urgent receptivity. He said, "My guy, it ain't the dealer's fault. He didn't create the game, he just lives in it. You need to tell your boy to quit playing and get sober. An addict has to make that choice. You stop one dealer, an addict will find ten more. It's why I'm rich."

Hearing it stung, but it was true.

Have you ever been there? Afraid to look truth in the face? Ownership can be painful. But beautiful. There is something freeing about owning anything. Even something small. Like a decision. Like a work ethic. Ownership breeds ownership. Don't get caught swinging at things that are not really the problem. Like a wise street legend once said, "Don't hate the player, hate the game."

I have taken that one step further in my life: I won't hate the players, but I *also* won't hate the game. If I don't like something that I see? I'll just change the game altogether.

Maybe the time is up for you too, to tolerate things you don't actually have to live with. There are so many decisions in front of you right now that you can maximize and change. Focus on those. Then watch how the rest start to fall in line.

———

I recently sat with a single mom of three rapidly growing teenage boys. She had been divorced now for years, but the effects of her verbally abusive husband were still very active and very real. As many people know, when you divorce a spouse but still must co-parent the children from the marriage, there is no "clean break" from that person. Our friend was still hearing damaging words from this man, often in front of her sons, and her boys have now slowly started to emulate that which they see: disrespect toward women.

You could hear the resignation in her voice as she told me, "It's just normal for me. To be told I'm worthless. To be told I'm an idiot. It must feel normal for my boys, because that's all they have ever known or seen." I told her that it is in fact not normal to acclimate oneself to dysfunction. Which is what happens when you are around unhealthy people for so long: You become unhealthy yourself. You accept and tolerate things simply because they have persisted for so long.

We agreed that the cycle had to stop, and it began with this amazing woman believing that she was really worthy of honor and respect. Step one for her? Refusing to allow words to be thrown at her that were unacceptable—from her ex-husband, from her sons, and even from her own inner dialogue.

The road to health starts with ownership. The word *victim* looks really similar to the word *victory*. Amazing how a few letters, a few choices moved around here and there, can lead to an entire new definition and destination.

own the chapter

The mirror is a dangerous thing. If you're feeling good, it's your friend. But if you don't like what you see, it can be an enemy you avoid because it's too hard to face. Displaced blame can disrupt your entire destiny. Is it possible that you have put the focus on the wrong things in certain challenges? Do you have broken relationships because you are consumed with the wrongs somebody else committed and you have failed to own your part in the matter? The only person who you can truly control in this life is yourself. Although it doesn't solve every problem, focusing on you sometimes—and what you can do better—can bring you peace while you wait for others to get their acts together. Rather than being critical and *looking out*, where can you be constructive and *look in* to bring change in your life? Less blame and more ownership leads to the fruitful life we all desire.

Chapter Twenty-Four

If You're Racist and You Know It, Clap Your Hands

I DON'T THINK LIVING IN a racist, bigoted world is something that we have to accept. I don't care how nasty the fight is or will become, how many times we have to stand up to what's wrong so we can shout about what's right. I actually believe that there are more rational, humble, peace-loving, and peace-promoting people in this world than there are racist, ignorant, and hurtful people. The issue is where the power lies. It doesn't matter how many good people there are in this world; if the power structures are created by and protected by those who make the calls and hold the cards, things won't change.

But I still believe that there are enough people ready to

truly own this issue, and we can see drastic change in our lifetime. That's why we are literally in a race—to reach more people, help more people, educate more people quicker than ever before, so we can see more change than we have seen. Racially speaking, are things better? Yes. But that statement is like saying, "If you have been shot ten times before and recently have only been stabbed five times, are you in better shape?" The issue is constant attack, not different types of pain.

I knew it was bad in our country. I grew up in Virginia, many of my closest friends are black, and my best friend throughout junior high and high school—and still to this day—is Korean. So my perspective on what it's like to be a minority in America has been heavily broadened due to hearing their stories and seeing their lives play out in front of me. I will never know what it's like to be a minority in our country, though I can earnestly try to keep my eyes and ears open to see and hear challenges from others' lives. I can continually try to become more aware. Awareness often can be the stepping-stone to real activism. Once you know about something, you're accountable for what you do about that something. So when it comes to racism, I always try to help people be more aware that racism runs much deeper than they may think; hits closer to home than they may think; and might even be in the mirror they look at every day.

I'll never forget listening to a genuinely naive friend of mine unwittingly give himself away as a truly unaware white man. He said, "All this talk about racism—it's not even real anymore! Things have changed. Most professional athletes are black!" For one, obviously, this is a stupid thing to say in general. But at least my friend was trying to engage. I told him, "Okay, so let's talk about the NFL. You love the NFL. Let's say roughly eighty percent of the league is black. How many owners of teams are black?" He couldn't answer.

I told him I would up the challenge. I said, "Matter of fact, let's take the three major sports in America. Ninety-two teams in all. You know how many black principal owners there are? *One.* Does that seem odd to you?" He agreed that it did.

I took it back to his beloved NFL and asked him how many black head coaches he thought there were, considering that the league is dominated by black players. He said, "Well, there have to be a lot, I'm sure." I told him that in 2017, the number of minority coaches in the league was at an all-time high: eight. *Eight.* In fact, the NFL was so systematically racist that it had to actually institute a rule that ensured black candidates for head coaching jobs would get interviews. Not the job, mind you—just interviews. Is this because white coaches are better? Obviously not, as year after year coaches who are absolutely notably unsuccessful get chance number three or four, while black coaches walk out of interviews without getting the main job.

You know what my friend said? "I wasn't aware. But things are better. I mean, they have their own television station, called BET. We don't have a station called White Entertainment Television, do we?"

I told him that in fact we do. It's called every other TV station.

This conversation kept landing on the same phrase: My friend said repeatedly, "I was not aware." Maybe that was true. But awareness is actually a choice. My children, for instance, are aware of racial disparity in our country. Last Christmas, my daughter Ava turned to me after a commercial for the nonstop marathon showing of the movie *Home Alone* that happens during the holidays and said, "Dad, why do they call this movie 'an American classic'? There is one black person in this movie. That's not America."

Awareness, my friends, comes from environment and intention. That moment with Ava encouraged me a little bit. But the reality is that we have a really long way to go when it comes to owning this sinful problem and advocating for real change.

This was made clear to me again when I made a statement at church that produced about as much vitriol and hate and anger toward me and toward our church as anything I have said to date.

The statement I made was: "Black lives matter."

It's important to note the context in which I made this statement. NYC was in a state of unrest. Throughout our country there had been a rash of very public, very painful, very troubling cases of situations between police and black men. Things were heightened greatly due to the Eric Garner situation because this happened in New York City; it was caught on film, and the aftermath played out in front of the nation.

I personally was troubled by the entire climate. And in our church, diversity is more than a goal. It's a value. Due to this, we have an extremely diverse congregation, and I knew that I had to say something about what was going on. Racism in our country was not constructed in a day, and I knew whatever meager offering I was going to bring was not going to solve any problems.

That was not even my goal. My goal was to bring attention to a part of our society that was hurting. That was fearful. That was in overt pain and frustration. Bring attention to the simple fact that we need to rally together and stand with those we love.

But the closer it got to Sunday, the more annoyed and almost perplexed I got about the reaction from people on these issues. The Black Lives Matter movement had been getting tons of press. It was extremely polarizing coverage, and I knew many people who genuinely didn't know a lot about this movement or what it stood for; and really, that wasn't remotely my concern: I didn't intend to focus on this. My irritation and frustration centered around what I was reading in the press and on social media from *white people*. It was unfathomable to me. Any time somebody would say, "Black lives matter," somebody else would counter with, "Yes, but *all* lives matter." I couldn't believe people could be this anti-logic and anti-compassion. Whether that was the motive is irrelevant. We can't know people's hearts. We can, however, feel the impact of people's actions and words, and it was clear this was becoming an increasingly toxic conversation in general. Apparently people found it very difficult to separate a sentence from a movement. It was as if suddenly a statement had lost its stand-alone meaning due to an association with something else. This would be the equivalent of people making it impossible to say "just do it" without others saying, "You support Nike. Nike makes shoes in Third World countries. You support sweat shops." When in fact, no, you were really just saying "just do it" to your tattoo artist after thirty minutes of deliberating about getting one or not. The moment anybody would say "Black lives matter," people would usually counter with, "That movement is racist too. They hate cops." (Both stupid and false allegations.)

I kept telling anybody who would listen: Movements have their own statements. We can still say this sentence, even if you take issue with a certain movement that uses it frequently: Black lives matter. It doesn't need to be qualified. It doesn't need to be countered. Either they do . . . or they do not. And people in our black community feel so strongly that much of America feels they do not, so that statement became a rallying cry.

One irate person confronted me after some post I made on Instagram and said, "You need to educate yourself on that movement. You have *no idea* what they are about. You are a fool to speak on things you don't know about." Little did she know that Opal Tometi, one of the original three who actually founded the movement, was a faithful part of our church for over four years. I knew more about this movement than most people did firsthand. But we live in a "shoot first, ask questions last" culture—literally—and it ends bad on the streets and in conversation. I told her, "Thanks, I'll be sure to do that." And I shook my head.

So on Sunday, I spoke about peace, I spoke about love, and I spoke about empathy. Which apparently is a word some people have never heard. Ever. The easiest and quickest way to get to the heart of the word is in its literal definition. It means "to sit in the path of." That's it. My request to our church was simple: empathy first, opinion second, if warranted. Meaning before you get on your soapbox of belief, simply walk into the path of the person who is communicating and sit on that path. Look at things from that view. Hear things from that view. Process things from that view. After you have done that? Almost always your tone at minimum changes. Perhaps your opinion remains, but the spirit with which you give it is drastically different.

I asked our church to empathize with those they don't know. Imagine you lost your father or best friend in the middle of a very dicey, questionable, tragic situation—and it appeared nobody would be held accountable for that. Would you want people to tell you how to feel? Would you want people to tell you that what you feel and see is actually wrong? Of course you wouldn't. Once we have empathized, we have listened, we have mourned, we have leaned on each other? Sure. Let's try to be constructive. We can't forget, though, that the best constructive conversations are opened up through the door of compassion and empathy. It's been said that "People don't care how much you know until they know how much you care." It needs to be said more, because it's never been more true.

This seems pretty simple, right? You would be wrong to assume that. Because what I said that really bothered people was this: "At our church, we are not going to be saying 'All lives matter' concerning the issues of police brutality and race right now. Because *of course* we all believe this. This does not need to be mentioned. Right now? It would appear by any account that on our streets black lives matter less. Until we see change, I will use this phrase, I will support those who feel the need to say that, and I believe there is still hope for us to cling to as a society. This statement does not belong to any movement. Nobody has exclusive rights to grammar and words. So when I say it, I'm speaking to that phrase. I am not condemning or supporting *any* organization right now."

I remember thinking, *That was mild. But at least it was something, and I need to say more.* I found out that I had said plenty. Tweets, hate mail, and literal death threats to me and my family came in. Quite a few, actually.

And that's when I knew we were going to win this fight. Because if it was that easy to prove how ridiculous people's thinking really was, there was nowhere to go but up. Not all people who are misguided are evil and stupid. Quite often it's just a case of lack of exposure to knowledge that we take for granted. Putting yourself in a position to be aware of views, feelings, and experiences costs you nothing except your comfort. But sometimes being aware that you have been unaware can be the best kind of uncomfortable—because it makes a position change vital.

───────────

One sincere person talked to me in my office about this that week and said, "But Pastor Carl, all lives matter. You can't separate 'black lives.'" I told this person, "Imagine if you are running a fundraising marathon for the fight against cancer. Worthy cause, right? Well, imagine on every corner somebody running up to you, in your face, yelling, 'But diabetes matters too! Diabetes kills people too!' Wouldn't that be stupid? Wouldn't you say to that person, 'Yes. Of course. But right now we are focusing on cancer.' Is that okay?"

She said, "Yes, but what about the police? It seems like you are anti-police."

I told her that was asinine logic as well. I said, "You don't have to be anti-anything just because you are fighting for something else. You don't have to be anti-police just because you are anti-injustice. Being passionate about one thing does not have to be an immediate disparagement to another. I love the many heroes, truly, who make up so much of our police force. They have an almost impossible job. I pray for them daily. But no profession, ever, should be without reform and accountability and serious investigation when people feel this threatened. Especially when the decisions they make hold life-or-death consequences."

For whatever reason, that illustration got through to this person. The response I got? "I had never thought about it like that."

I told her lovingly, "Glad to have you on the good ship called *Logic*. Plenty of room!"

If more people could just say that, we could take some serious ground on some serious issues. So in the middle of all the tension, all the controversy, I sat in a coffee shop later that day with a sense of resilience. Because this fight is winnable. If you and I can take a moment and consider others, genuinely, and choose to put our own views and our own opinions down for just a little while? We can slowly but surely find answers for so very many things.

About a week later, I challenged our church to "handle their own business" before trying to opine or get anybody else to change their business. I said to look in the mirror and talk to your own families. You might not be able to change the world. But you can change yourself. You can change your own house.

I went home after church, and I grabbed all three of my kids and Laura, and I sat down and we had a family meeting. I asked them, "Have you heard anything at school about Black Lives Matter?" They all said yes, except for Roman, who said, "Dad, I love Black Panther. Do you want to go outside and play?" Roman was dismissed from the meeting.

Charlie said, "Dad, I actually made a shirt that says 'Black Lives Matter,' and I was going to wear it, but somebody said I was racist if I do."

I said, "Girl, you wear your shirt. Although you're only ten, you are a leader. You tell people when they question you that if the answer to the question on your shirt is yes, nothing more needs to be said—that you are simply stating that black lives matter."

She said, "Cool, Dad. Because they do."

Ava concurred, and we all prayed together. When we were done, Charlie had tears in her eyes and she said, "Dad, is PJ going to be okay?" PJ is one of my best friends on Earth. He is black, and has become a de facto uncle to my children due to the sheer time spent at my house over six years.

I said, "Yes, baby. Why?"

She said, "I just see men his color always on the news, and bad things are happening to them."

I assured her that PJ was going to be okay, and that's

exactly the reason we work as hard as we do—to stand strong in what we believe. My goal as her father includes teaching her to think right. To not allow fear to dictate feelings. And it's not just a good lesson for Charlie. It's a good reminder for all of us.

Why are we so fearful of dialogue? Why are we so fearful, so defensive, when presented with views we do not always share? I will echo until the day I die that empathy, that love, does not always mean "advocacy." Not at all. The Black Lives Matter movement is a great microcosm of our culture. There are things to love, things to admonish, things to agree with. There very well may be things to not take on board. Things to not get behind. But whoever said you had to agree with every single thing about anything? I'm pretty sure I don't even agree with myself about me often.

The point is to search for ways *to* agree. Search for ways *to* love. It's a much more fascinating and fulfilling way to live. I want to continue to own what I can in matters like racism, bigotry, tension in culture.

I'm not telling you that you are wrong and that you see things incorrectly. I'm asking you to take a moment and ask yourself, "*Could* I be wrong? Have I looked at this from an angle I wouldn't naturally see?" That is where a mind-set shift begins. That's where change begins. So many people are focused on changing what they do. That can be helpful, without a doubt. But not as many people are focused on changing what they think. And what they think is causing what they do. So it makes sense for all of us to take a long look and to think about these issues that are not going away anytime soon.

This is where change either lives or dies. Right between the eyes. That thing we call our mind is either a weapon of mass construction and hope, or one of mass destruction and loss. I know what I want my mind to represent.

A few nights ago, I said goodbye to some friends who left my house after watching some basketball on TV. I walked them to the door and said goodbye to both. To my friend JT, who is white, I said, "See you later. You owe me money. Love you." To PJ, I said, "See you later. You owe me money too. Love you. Text me when you get home safe, okay?"

I shut the door and thought about what I just said—that was as natural and normal to me as ever—and why I had to say it. We have a long way to go, absolutely. And I reserve the right to believe passionately we are going to get there. Together. One mind-set shift at a time. We need to remain aware that systems, no matter how entrenched they seem, are breakable. They are changeable. I don't care how long a system has been running—whether it's a system of thinking or a system of racism or bigotry, it can be changed.

In fact, more than anything else, our last two presidential elections should reawaken our awareness to this fact. The political system failed two times in a row. We elected a black president in a system that made that reality virtually impossible. For a black man from Chicago to push through countless systematic ceilings and barriers and win? Impossible. But Barack Obama broke the system. This past year, our country elected Donald Trump. In a system that was supposedly created to never, ever allow somebody who some believe is "part of the 1 percent" to preside over the common 99 percent, he won. For a man with zero political experience to win the office of president? Impossible. Yet he broke the system too.

This leaves you and me no excuse for not believing that we can force change in any area. That we too can live with awareness that drives us to realize it's never too late to change— change ourselves, change our surroundings, and, who knows? Maybe change the world we live in, day by day.

So when people tell me "Carl, eradicating racism is impossible," forgive me if I disagree. I'm too aware of what I see around me.

own the chapter

Racism and prejudice affect us all. Either we have been the perpetrators of it or the victims of it, sometimes even both. The first step to making sure we are a part of the answer and not the problem is to simply acknowledge that we need to consider the possibility. Much of racism and bigotry is so deep-seated through culture and often heritage, we have unwittingly developed mentalities that perhaps we didn't intend to cultivate. It's not an affront to your character or dignity to admit you may have some issues you need to investigate in your own way of thinking. It *is* an indictment of character to avoid the issue and pretend you have been unaffected. Nobody should have to "walk a mile" in another's shoes to have empathy, because we all have our own shoes. Our own stories we wish others would consider before judgment is cast. May we all endeavor to be better, kinder people. If we can, the world we live in can look much different.

Chapter Twenty-Five

Culture, in Three Acts

"CULTURE."

It's a word used so often, in so many ways, you can't take for granted that everybody knows what it is and what it does. The definition of culture that I believe is most accurate is "a particular form or stage of civilization, as that of a certain nation or period." Culture has a language, culture has a voice, culture has a community. And without a doubt culture has its casualties.

This is such an important topic that I will temporarily break from typical book flow and split this chapter into three acts. As in a Broadway show that has three major parts. Because each matters in accordance with the other, and culture is very similar to a play or show you might go to see. You pay to watch it, and if you like it enough you start living like the show you like the most. The world around us has so much to do with what is going on inside us that to not actively learn, prepare, protect, or maximize its effects, depending on which way you lean, is a one-way ticket to irrelevancy and desensitization to the basic human condition.

Act One: Molly Percocet

Whether you know or not, culture has impacted you. It's affected you. And there is a good chance that you didn't even see it coming, because "culture" is coy like that. It's so almost passive in its pervasiveness. We don't particularly appreciate air, for instance. It's everywhere. We breathe it, we need it, who cares about air. Until you find out the air you have been breathing is killing you. Then? Air becomes important. Suddenly, you have to take account for it.

"Dad, I don't understand. I like Future. He's a cool rapper and his songs are fun to dance to."

Ava was making her case as to why she didn't mind dancing with her friends to a rapper who has become, for now, a culture creator. Future is no doubt unique. He dresses different. He says what he feels and, to most people, his music sounds good. It's that kind of methodical beat production that almost puts you in a trance and, before you know it, your head is moving to this beat and you might even sing a line or two without realizing you knew the words.

So when I heard Ava sing some lines of Future's smash hit "Mask Off" that go like this—*Percocets, Molly, Percocets . . . Chase a check, never chase a b*tch*—my "dad radar" went into overdrive.

All cultures have subcultures that impact the greater cultural bottom line, some more and some less than others. The hip-hop culture? Please. For my money, it remains one of the premier touch points for understanding the state of our union. Hip-hop is not a thermometer. It is a thermostat. Always has been. If you are one of those people who still tries to dismiss this, good luck with that, and do so at your own peril. Research what happened when hip-hop culture began to speak in many ways for people in urban communities who felt they had no voice. Things changed.

For the good it has done, like all flipsides, the bad is just as severe. One negative in particular has been its ability to make misogyny sound acceptable and even appealing. Hip-hop icon Tupac Shakur laid this out in bright lights, as he had a smash hit called "Dear Mama" and another called "Keep Ya Head Up" that honored women in his community and moms who were heroes. Yet he also produced other smash hits like "I Get

Around," literally doing the polar opposite. On the one hand, we honor you. On the other, we actually hate you and have chosen to devalue you every chance we get.

This hypocrisy is not unique to the hip-hop culture, let me tell you. Church culture at its worst has done more damage, and I'll get to that later. The point is that if you don't know what matters to you in this life? Culture—which is confused in its very essence because it's a collection of voices, opinions, subsets and systems created and propagated by flawed humanity—will be happy to tell you what to stand for. And who to be. And what to do.

And that's the problem.

I have no issue when culture tells me how to wear my socks. Up or down or no socks at all. I have a huge issue when culture tries to tell me how to navigate my soul.

So back to Ava and Future. I told Ava what I try to tell her in a lot of matters that may seem little but represent much more.

"You are going to need to see this for yourself, so let me tell you why I'm concerned tonight."

Keep in mind, parenting has its own culture. Laura and I reject the notion that we need to demonize things in order to protect our kids from them. You should too. If you freak out every time something comes the way of your child and run from it and hide them, please believe the moment they are able they will go explore exactly what it was that bothered Mom and Dad so much. We also equally reject the, "Learn for yourself, child. You tell me what you want to do." Lord help us. My children do not live in a democracy. They live in my kingdom. They do what I say until they pay bills. But I still want them to learn why I run my kingdom/our home like I do.

So I broke it down for her. I said, "Do you know what Molly is? Do you know what Percocet is? Do you know what he means by 'chase a check'?"

Ava honestly didn't know. So I told her. What those drugs do. Why people take them. What it means when men call women things like Future[1] calls women. I told her that thinking that demeans women, oppresses women. It's not always going to be overt. Sometimes it's slick. It's cool. It will even be defended. I told her that as it stands now? Women can do the same work that men do, but they won't get paid the same for it. Often *better* work. I asked her if that sounded right.

She said, "No way! How does that happen?!"

As you can see, one question about culture is going to lead to more. I told Ava, "I'm not going to tell you you can't listen to Future. I am going to teach you about culture. Because culture is not king in this house or in your life. Know what you

---

[1]Who, by the way, can do whatever he wants. This isn't a shot at him. It's just a dad explaining his language to his daughter.

dance to. Know what you put into your soul. If you honestly do that, I can live with your decisions."

We talked for a long time that night, and it's something that needs to be talked about a lot more with adults. Because culture is killing us. And it's not going anywhere. As much as I would like to put an ankle-length dress on Ava and an old school bonnet and make sure her long legs never see the light of day and move up to a small cabin in rural Idaho and keep her safe, that's not her calling. She is on this earth to be a leader. So we have to start planning now, to be "in it but not of it."

I believe that the more we talk about complicated culture moments, the clearer things can get. How we think and talk about it matters so much. I cling to a passage in my Bible out of Romans, which was written to people dealing with this exact crisis-of-culture-type tension:

Do not conform to the way of this world, but be transformed by the renewing of your mind.

How, you might ask, do we do this? Stick with me.

Act Two: Nobody Cares about Your Truth

Romans 8 goes on to say, "then you will know God's will." This is a loaded scripture, and its application and ramifications are explosive. The implication is that there is, in fact, a plan. Not a trend, but an actual path to adhere to. Inherently, this becomes pop culture's number one nemesis. As its name suggests, pop culture swings, depending on what's hot and what's not. This is not always a bad thing. But when it comes to matters that affect us all, this is an important variable to factor in our life navigational settings. Imagine putting your destination in your phone, being certain about it, only to have Siri keep saying "rerouting" every five minutes. This is culture.

Right now, what is "superhot" is a trend that can be best described as "backlash to boxes." Meaning labels we put on people, or boxes we force people to fit into—from race to religion to sexuality to political persuasion—are literally blowing up. If this was treated with some context and rational thinking, this doesn't have to be a bad thing. In fact, maybe it's needed at times. I can't count the number of times people have said to me, "Well, you don't look the way a pastor should look."

But culture doesn't love common sense at all. So we swing to extremes, give whatever cause or moment we are passionate about a cool slogan and maybe even a #hashtag, and now it becomes "a thing." How many times have you heard some type of the following: "No labels. Don't you dare label me." Or, "Don't draw lines around me. I wanna live outside the lines. Lines create division." Shoot, we could easily spin this real quick and make it a chant, make it a march. I can see it now: "No boxes, no lines! I'm gonna get what's mine! No boxes, no lines! I'm gonna get what's mine!" I would probably buy that T-shirt.

The problem is it's totally stupid. Let's walk it out for a moment, you who may want "no labels." You don't want labels? Okay, fine. I'm going to pour rat poison in one bottle, and I'm going to pour water in another bottle. I'm going to put them both in front of you, in nondescript bottles with no labels. Now do you care about labels? You bet your life (literally) you do. Labels are not the enemy. The intent *behind* the labels could be a problem—perhaps the label makers might need shifting—but we can't just throw out labels.

Culture, if it is your compass, will lead you astray in every single way. It's meant to be used. It cannot be something that continually uses *you*. Can you imagine a face that had no lines? No shapes that vary? It would be impossible to distinguish it from any other face. In the attempt to create more uniqueness you would have eliminated the very core of uniqueness itself.

I want to be a part of culture *changing*. Not another person who is conforming to whatever wind the culture is blowing. To truly do this, you simply have to know who you are. So other people, other cultures can stop telling you.

This leads me to perhaps my biggest irritation of pop culture today, and I can sum it up with one phrase that you have absolutely heard:

"I want to live my truth."

Allow me to practice what I preach for a moment and give this proper context. Not everybody who says this means the same thing. Sometimes I have heard it said in a way where people simply mean to do what you feel strongly about. Be yourself. Be different if need be. To a degree, sure. I can live with that. But what this becomes is a monster. And this monster has a voracious appetite and is currently eating any- and everything in its path. Loosely translated, living my truth really means, "I shall do whatever the hell I want to do, regardless of what it does to you." And under this guise of "living my truth," people are doing what they have always done: hurting other people. It might not seem like that or even start like that. But that is irrelevant. Where something finishes is what defines it.

On the surface, it sounds very nice. Very holistic. "Live your truth, bro. Totally. And I'll live mine. Let's go protest anybody who doesn't agree." Firstly, this is a self-defeating argument. What if my truth *is* defying your truth? How do we know who's wrong? Secondly, I couldn't care less about your truth if it destroys my life. So to pretend that the "live your truth" mantra is helpful is in fact the opposite.

If you are reading this and you're uncomfortable, hear *my* truth for a second. If living our truth is going to be our culture backbone—and believe me, people want it to be—we have to walk this out. I have to respect your truth? If you say it, no matter what it is, I have to roll with it or risk being called "oppressive"? So you can wake up tomorrow and tell me that you are black or white, tall or short, male or female—you can literally make up your identity and I have to live with that?

Well, since we have no lines, I can't ask where to draw the line. But if we did, what if you decide your truth is to walk into my house, take my TV and my shoes and claim them as your own. I have to live with that? Guess what your truth is going to get you? A whole lot of trouble.

This is key when it comes to cultural baselines that we accept. We can't apply them in isolation. So we want "our truth" when it suits us. But the problem arises when your truth isn't truth at all, and you try to force me to believe it. Or at least deal with it. I'm not on the my truth train, and I don't think you should be, either.

So where does that lead us? To a mind-blowing idea that will draw lines all around your life:

LIFE. IS. NOT. ABOUT. YOU.

If that was truly "our truth," imagine what kind of culture we would live in. Instead, we are promoting things like "Go on a self-discovery journey. Find your truth." I've got some bad news about that. A self-discovery journey is a waste of time. Let me save you some miles. It's going to lead you to the exact same place. Back to yourself—a flawed, broken human being who has inherent deficiencies.

My opinion matters, sure. What I like and what I want and how I see things, yes, they hold value. But when it gets down to it? I'm not God. And the nasty truth about the "my truth" momentum of culture? That's exactly, ultimately, what people want to be. We want to run our own show. We want to dictate our own lives. We want to call our own shots. If you are a proponent of this thinking, let me ask you: how's that working out for you? Or even more important, how's that working out for those around you?

───────────

Laura and I sat down once with a woman who I considered a close friend for a long time. Our families hung out, she loved her kids, loved life, was (and is) a fun person to be around. We agreed on a lot. Except on this day.

She told me very matter-of-factly, "I am going to leave my husband, and I'm going to get a divorce." We had been aware that they had had some marriage problems that had ebbed and flowed for as long as we have known them. But they always sought help. They always tried to get better. We had not realized she had changed that course. I asked her why—and also why she was so definitive with me without leaving room for anything I might have to say.

She said, "I just don't want to try anymore. Marriage is not for me. I'm sure it will be hard on the kids, and my husband. He's a good man for sure. But I don't think marriage suits me. It's time for me to live my truth."

So for the record, she admitted this decision would drastically hurt her children. Would crush her husband. Would break her vows. But in her words, "her truth" was the main priority. There was nothing we could offer her that made any difference. My friend and her truth walked out on her family. This is not a judgment of her. It's simply a factual account and a real-time illustration of where our culture of "my truth" leads "us."

I believe with all my heart there is a better option. There is a culture-defying, culture-overcoming, culture-protected way to root our lives so that this type of thinking—while innocent in some parts but deadly in most—does not destroy the very things we are trying to build.

It begins with this statement: There is a higher truth.

This will be debated. This will be picked apart—not just in this book but everywhere. It has been, forever. But when you start seeking a higher truth, you begin to realize how small "my truth" really is.

"My truth" about people is that I don't like a lot of them and would be perfectly happy to let some people run right off the cliff they are headed toward. But every day I want my truth to die, because it begins and ends with me. I want to live for more than what I want. Yes, it's hard. Yes, it means lines will be drawn. But I refuse to accept the notion that my way is the right way.

If you picked up this book, maybe you know where I'm headed with where to find "the higher truth." And you're right. I do believe in God. I do believe in and read the Bible. I do believe that Jesus Christ really lived, and He really died, and He really rose again so that people like me would not have to live enslaved to the crushing patterns of this broken world. But I choose to believe what I believe for the exact same reasons people choose to not believe it.

I heard somebody say to me, "All roads lead to heaven, Carl. Just because it's good for you doesn't mean it's for everybody. All roads, not one road. What a narrow way to think. It's actually offensive."

I told this person what I will tell you right now: If we can all agree that a collection of our own personal truths being the moral, mercy, justice, and love standard for life sounds like the worst idea ever, we have to agree that it also means perhaps there is a higher truth out there we have to find. Which means there is right. And there is wrong. So when Jesus said, "I am the way, the truth, and the life. Nobody gets to the Father except through me," maybe what seems to be an immovable line of division is actually a line of truth so clear, so radiant that we have to *choose* to walk away from it.

People say, "Love has no lines." This makes zero sense. Because to know what love is you have to also call out what love is not. That's exactly what Jesus did. We can take it or leave it, and I have made my choice to believe it. To follow Jesus, literally step one means to eradicate the "my truth" from your life. My desires I have to put to death. My wants, my happiness are not my driving force. God's promise is that as I die to "my truth," I day by day begin forming my life, my identity into His truth and His will. You know what happens? My truth starts to line up with what Jesus said. How He lived. And if I ever get confused? I walk my truth right up to what God said. And if they don't match up, guess which one has to go?

Here is the good news for those immediately drawing lines on me, even though you profess to hate lines: My truth is a good one. It doesn't affect you adversely. True Christianity is most likely not what you have seen portrayed on TV. (Hello again, culture!) True Christianity is to admit you are a sinner. To dedicate your life to honoring God. To help others before you help yourself. To not force your beliefs on anybody but to live them so well people *want* to know what you have. To love people so much you're even willing to walk away from them out of love rather than say nothing and be a silent advocate during their demise. It means to help the needy, from the famous to the faceless, and it means to be willing to die for what Jesus said was truth. To fight for justice. To accept the forgiveness of God freely, and continue to change daily. "My truth," ultimately, is to serve others for the rest of my life, with my life. So if I am wrong? I missed well.

Yet I don't think I am wrong, because I didn't land on this truth so I could "live a good life on Earth." No way. I follow Jesus because there is eternity to think about as well—what happens after this good or bad life is over. Culture is not going to point you to that. No way. Culture isn't going to save your life or transform your soul. Culture, in fact, is no God at all, despite what we make it out to be.

My hope isn't necessarily for you to believe what I believe. My hope is that you look at what drives you. What shapes you. What fuels you and what guides you. Are you changing culture? Or is culture changing you? Are you influencing? Or are you "under the influence"?

Look at it.

Own it.

It's not too late to draw a line. It's not too late to define what success looks like and what it doesn't. It's not too late to label people with grace rather than hate.

But whatever you do, don't just "Go with the flow." Pick a direction and go all in. Just make sure you are willing to bet your life on it. Because "the truth" is? You are. Every day.

Act Three: Brick Killed a Guy

I couldn't live with myself if I wrote a book and didn't have one reference to *Anchorman*. Will Ferrell is a genius, the movie is a classic, and if you don't think so I don't care because it's my truth and I'm sticking to it.

There is an epic scene where the rival broadcast teams get into an old-school brawl that escalates to medieval-era violence. It's hilarious, and my favorite part of the scene is when they are all talking about the fight afterward and Ron Burgundy says, "Yeah, Brick killed a guy. You might want to hide out for a while." They don't know who he killed—Brick, played by Steve Carrell, sure didn't know. But somebody definitely died.

It reminds me of what it looks like when we "fight culture"

the wrong way, in order to live the right way. We don't know exactly what we are fighting. Perhaps we don't even know *why* we are fighting. But we are surely fighting. And casualties are strewn all over.

This plays out all the time in New York City. You can at times see two different movements protesting each other, but nobody is winning because they are both ultimately doing the same thing. They are fighting . . . about fighting. During the election in which we saw Donald Trump become our 45th president of the United States, this was a vivid reality. I saw people holding up signs that said "I'm with her. I hate him" face-to-face with others who had signs that said "If you love America, you love Donald. Plain and simple. If you don't, you hate it." Hate on both sides.

You know who lost that war? Logic. Peace. Reasonable conversation. This is what happens in a world or culture that lacks direction. You fight. But there is a huge chance you may be fighting the wrong thing.

Enter Church Culture as a shiny beacon of illustrative light.

I am intimately involved in this one, let me tell you! Church culture tends to pride itself on *not* being a part of the culture. Which becomes its own weird subculture. When I say church culture, you know what I mean. Where we make up rules God has no idea about. Where we say things are doctrinal when in fact they are traditional and completely optional—yet if you don't adhere to them, God is against you. Stuff like that.

I remember one time praying for two young men who were fantastic and very humbly said, "Pastor, can you pray for us?"

I said of course, and as I went to pray they took their hats off. And I said, "Hey, wait a minute. Why did you do that?"

They said, "Well, I grew up in a church that said it was disrespectful to pray with a hat on, and that God doesn't like it."

I said, "My friend, no disrespect intended to wherever you came from, but do you realize we are praying to Jesus? You know, the man who died naked and humiliated on a cross so guys like us could someday know what grace feels like? Put your hat on. I'm positive that God is not intimidated by your New Era lid. That is a tradition in some places. Cool. Not here. I will not pray until you put your hat *on*."

Imagine a church culture that kicks people out for having a hat on. Rather than fight to help the person who is trying to actually get help, let's rage against hats!

No thanks. I don't want to fight culture by being fearful of culture, and then in turn create more culture that makes the problem worse. I want to fight the right way. And the best way to influence our world and not fall victim to it? Know your convictions—your "yes, I wills" and your "no, I won'ts." That way you won't get seduced by the much easier and lazy way of living, which is to rage against a machine that isn't the actual threat. You get to look like you're making a difference when in fact you are doing nothing.

I think our church in NYC is a really good example of a group of people who are passionately connected and committed to a shared set of convictions that has led us to see a whole lot of conversions, despite some church culture attacks that are actually unintentionally funny in hindsight.

A few years ago, rumors of the "Illuminati" was a trendy thing. Who was in it, what was it, just how much of our world was controlled by it. And since our church has a really big platform and influential reach, that comes with a target on our back that is just as big as it seems. It's part of the territory, and we have seen and heard it all. Our culture in general is so warped by disappointment that we don't see something that is working and think, "That's awesome." We see something that is effective and lean toward, "It's fishy. Something must be up. No way can Hillsong actually be the real deal. Too many people go. They have too much fun. Something is off, for sure. Let's go blog about it." And off they go.

At one point, I kept hearing things about our church being affiliated with the Illuminati. Over and over. I posted a photo once of me holding up a peace sign at my son's birthday party, and in a matter of minutes I saw in my comments, "See! Told you. Illuminati. That's an Illuminati hand signal." After a few weeks of this, it started to irritate me simply because I can never understand why people waste so much time trying to tear others down. If you don't like us? Fine. Go do it better, do it louder, and we will fade away. But our culture? That's too much work. We would rather get on somebody else's page and take some shots than step out into the real fight. But trolls are gonna troll. Such is life.

I finally had to say something when we had a conference at Madison Square Garden. To have a church meeting in the world's most famous arena, challenging people to love others and care about your neighbor and build our cities and fight for the voiceless is a miracle. After it ended, I was excited. And then I got a Google alert about a story talking about "Hillsong comes out in full Illuminati colors. Stage design proves it."

You know what our stage design was? A mountain. To represent Mount Zion. An iconic Biblical theme. And we had some cool neon triangles as well. Little did I know, the triangle was formed in hell. "Triangles are of the devil!"

My tipping point was when a very genuine person in our church asked sheepishly, "Pastor, *are* we a part of the Illuminati?"

I said, "Girl, please come Sunday." And somewhere in my message that day I took a moment to half in jest, half dead serious announce, "People of New York, now hear this. Shapes are shapes. A triangle is a triangle. We have not lost the right to use shapes because some people think a cult that in fact does not exist uses this shape. What's next? Are we going to protest geometry? Shall we stand outside of all American high schools and chant, 'No more shapes in math! No more shapes in math!' Of course not. Furthermore, let's stop fighting about the rainbow. The rainbow belonged to Noah way before the gay community put it on a flag and the University of Hawaii put it on their football helmets. The cross still means the cross. Even if a rapper who sings about murder wears one with diamonds on it. These things are what we make them. Can we please stop talking about this!"

Predictably, I received thunderous applause. I believe the world is still filled with incredibly smart, rational people who don't in fact want to waste a moment fighting the wrong fights. I urge people I love to, yes, be an advocate. Be active in what you believe. But do not miss the target. There are too many people getting caught in stupid cross fires. People are not the enemy. Fight for a principle, absolutely. Don't lose sight of our ultimate goal. Which is to win people, not divide them.

Which leads me back to Ava Lentz and Future.

After our talk, she said, "So, Dad, is Future bad?"

I told her, "My love, Future is a human being who makes music. He didn't force anybody to buy it or like it, and he is not the problem. We just don't agree with the content of the song. We don't have to go tell people, 'Future is bad.' What we can do is make music we love and plug it into the culture to give a better option. That takes work. But if you're up for it, I'm up for it. We can definitely pray for Future, though, 'cause he's just like us. Trying to find his way. Not to mention, his hair is incredible."

We went to get some ice cream after that, and enjoyed the instrumental version of the exact song in question. We loved it. After all, we can extract the parts of culture we like anytime we want. As long as we don't buy the whole thing every time.

That night we won a small victory against culture. We attacked no one, and our conversation led us to higher ground and some fresh ideas to reach more people. That's what happens when you fight the right fights. There is no collateral damage. Just collateral blessing. What a refreshing addition to culture that could be.

End of scene.

own the chapter

One of the best ways to determine the health of your own soul is to ask whether you are changing your environment or is your environment changing you. Have you had to adjust your standards to fit in? Or have you lived with such convictions people start rethinking their standards because of you? Typically, our language reveals this answer quickly. Sometimes we don't even realize when culture begins to invade so much of our lives, but our responses and conversations can let us know quickly where we are headed. My daughter walked in from school recently and said, "What's up, Bro." I said, "Excuse me?" She said, "Oh, Dad, all my friends call their dad 'Bro.' It's no big deal." I told her, "You're right, it's not a big deal. What *is* a big deal is respect and honor and people who will normally live up to your expectations of them. So if you want me to be 'Bro,' I can do that. Bros don't pay rent. They don't send you to summer camp. And they don't save money so someday you can go to college. I actually want to be 'Bro.'" This produced a quick semantic change in her. "Dad is good! Dad is good! I won't call you 'Bro'!" I could have let it slide, sure. But each moment you allow our world to influence you leads to another. And each moment you confront it and take inventory of it leads to another moment as well. Depends on which way you want to go in this life. To influence? Or to be influenced? I know which way I want to head. Do you?

Chapter Twenty-Six

In a Hurry to Nowhere

WATCHING PEOPLE IN TRAFFIC IS high on the unintentional comedy scale. I enjoy coming across the "party" car. You can't miss them. It's the crew that is stuck in traffic and figures "At least we are together so we might as well dance it out." And the music is blasting and they are having way more fun singing and laughing than you are watching them. There is the "divorce is near" car. The husband is blankly staring into the windshield almost as if he stares hard enough he might magically transport himself out of the car. Next to him is a wife who has that body language of vitriol, that wife cadence where you can tell she is saying things in short loud bursts, and right when you think she's done, more! And the husband stares forward again. You have the "I'm a star in my car" car, with the driver who is belting out a song that was never intended to be sung by said individual, but when in traffic their inner Whitney comes out.

My personal favorite, though, is the guy who is in such a manic hurry that he honks, punches the steering wheel, strains his neck outside every few minutes, and yells, "Come on! Come on! LET'S MOVE IT!" As if the other 43 million people in traffic are intentionally not moving and that guy is the *only* guy who has somewhere to be. The best part is when they weave in front of other people—when they see even a sliver of road daylight and slam on the accelerator and fly by you into another lane . . . only to be stuck right next to you again a few feet later. You feel like telling him, "Buddy, you know you are racing to the exact same red light that I'm cruising to as well?"

You have got to love people who race to stoplights. Until you realize that in life, not just traffic, we may be no better than Street Racer Steve. Rushing to go nowhere. Angry about moments in life that happen to us all. Frustrated with growth and processes of change that simply cannot be expedited.

I want to be in the party car. If it does me no good to "rush to a stop," maybe enjoying the ride going slower has some peace in its wisdom. I love the stretch of road in life where you can gooooooo. We all do. But it's just not realistic to think that we can live for those moments in our journey. We have to be able to slow down, take it all in, enjoy what's around, because most of our journey that matters is going to take a while.

"Go slower to get there faster."

A mentor of mine once told me that before my wife and I set out to plant and lead our church. It was one of those perfectly perplexing, paradoxical, yet peaceful wisdom drops that confuses you and totally makes sense at the same time. His wisdom for me was that I needed to be careful to realize that faster isn't better. That sometimes building something right, maximizing moments properly, takes time. And you end up getting there faster anyway, so you might as well enjoy what you are doing right now.

This is way easier said than done, however. Because the world we live in loves speed in general. Patience is no longer a virtue at all. So as a result we hate waiting for anything, ever. I love watching people freak out if things do not download fast enough on their smartphone. Forget the fact that we are receiving data from an invisible data cloud in a galactic atmosphere we can't see. If that thing takes more than one minute?

Many phones get assaulted physically. And it's revealing of some deeper issues for us. Waiting is not the enemy. In fact, it can be an asset.

I am what I like to call a "perpetual line-hopper." Meaning if I go to a store with multiple checkout lines, I find it *really* hard to stay in one. I am always sizing up that other line, way down the aisle, tracking its movement, trying to judge just how many items that person has in the "10 items or less" line. Is that eleven, possibly twelve? Do I need to notify a manager? All this runs through my mind as I wait.

I often cannot wait, so I bail on the line I am in and go hop in another line, even though my wife's unmistakable, semi-annoyed voice saying "I'm telling you, babe, this is gonna end up quicker, just stay here" plays loudly in my mind. Almost always, Laura is waiting for me in the car, peacefully hanging out with her items, as I come in twenty minutes later with my new story about how the line that looked shorter was in fact not at all and if I just would have waited where we were it would have paid off.

This is not just a "how to shop at Target" picture. Relationships that were headed somewhere have ended prematurely because somebody got impatient and tried to skip a line. Dreams that were coming to fruition stopped growing because a "quicker, better option" showed up and somebody couldn't resist.

Sometimes the slower, unspectacular line leads to the thing you're after. Shorter is not always better.

I have the honor and the privilege of officiating weddings for amazing couples in our church. And it's always funny to me how stressful wedding planning is, and then how quickly couples want the ceremony to be over. So I always gently propose a few moments that hopefully will press the slow-motion button on this precious day. Because the truth is, rarely do couples remember the DJ, the flower arrangements, the seating chart, the color of the cake. Most times they don't even remember saying the vows! So it's less a day where people get married and more a day that you "planned an event" and couldn't wait for it to end.

This is a danger in life. We are not put on this Earth to run from thing to thing, job to job, savings account to savings account, only to look back someday and question what impact we had, and search high and low to remember what happened. The opposite of "I was there" might be the dreaded "I missed the moment." Being intentional about slowing down and savoring this life is a huge step toward enjoying it.

But the second step has to be *engaging* in it. True engagement takes patience and presence. And these two things are apparently enemies to the Lentz DNA. I don't know how many projects I have started with joy. And left completely unfinished due to annoyance or unforeseen complications. And to compound this reality, I can see this same trait in my son.

We went to get Legos the other day, because I am a glutton for punishment. Let me just say: Whoever thought of Legos? Whoever can do Lego things with efficiency? Good for you. You're special. I didn't go to your Lego college, and we don't share the same gifts. Roman chose what looked like an awesome toy. It was a Lego fighter jet. The cover on the box was epic. We took it home and opened it up and immediately I think we both realized: *We have a problem.* I had never seen so many pieces. I have never seen a more complex diagram.

Roman gave up early and asked me to help. I could feel the pressure as his little eyes stared at me through his impossibly cute, thick prescription glasses. At one point I'm pretty sure they were fogging up as he realized: *Dad can't do Legos.* And he was right. I threw the box, I cursed the Legos, and I went and bought my boy some ice cream, hoping that the sugar rush would wash away this memory of failure from his father.

We came back later, and to my shock that same Lego fighter jet was assembled completely . . . and with accessories. I found out that if you did it correctly it could morph into a tank. And a car. My angelic friend who did this simply said, "Yeah, it's pretty easy, Carl. Takes a bit to follow the directions. But if you are patient, it makes sense."

I have never looked at Legos the same way. And really, some situations? I will think of that Lego moment and remember that if I can stick with this thing, this person, this job, not only will I get it done, I bet I can turn this into *more*.

———————

Do you have the patience to maximize the moment? It's worth it to stick with it.

own the chapter

It's frustrating when I see people who are in the same situation as I am, yet they seem to be enjoying so much more. It's like when you order something at a restaurant and you get it, look at what your friend has and immediately regret not ordering what they had. It's like you didn't see the option on the menu! I propose this could be the case in many aspects of life. We are at the same restaurant, looking at the same menu, we simply choose wrong sometimes. Are you constantly in a hurry? Do you feel like no matter how much you do, there is always so much more to do? This is a quick way to suck the enthusiasm and passion out of life. Peace is an option for you. Love is an option for you. Joy is an option for you. But you have to make the choices today to order those. There is no reason to envy another life when you have the right to access the same things they do.

Chapter Twenty-Seven

The Lies We Love

THE TRICKY THING ABOUT A good lie is that there is probably a shred of truth that has been delicately woven into the fabric of it, so you can't really tell that it's a lie.

"White people can't dance, bro. That's just a fact."

My friend was earnest in his delivery but misguided in his information. I told him clearly that _most_ white people can't dance. Big difference. It's just a subtle difference, but it changes everything. If it's true that white people can't dance, then why even try? But if it's not true? Dance on, white people. Dance on. There is hope.

This may not seem on its face like life-changing

information. The problem is that all of us will be faced with lies—about ourselves, about other people, about life in general—that may *appear* true sometimes but are in no way set in stone. Lies draw lines. And too often—like the chalk outlines around a dead body discovered by a detective in a dark alley somewhere—when you are surrounded by lies, they kill you.

Truth is our advocate in this life. But sometimes it helps to know what truth is *not* before we begin to discover what it is. This, however, is not as easy as it should be, because we live in a world right now where we cannot even trust the news we see on TV or the politicians we elect to protect what we hold dear. And our churches have not been spared, either. In fact, I have heard some of the best, most spiritual-sounding lies from professing Christians.

Since this is the lane of life I know the best, I will give you some examples of "the usual lie suspects" in and out of the church world. I know you have either heard these or maybe you even live according to one. I don't blame you because some of them sound pretty solid. But upon further review? A lie is a lie.

"God gives His toughest battles only to His strongest soldiers."

That's nice. I call this the *encouraging* lie. If you're going through some trials, this can make us feel like, "Okay, maybe God wants me to go through this." It's a lie. You won't find it in the Bible. God doesn't have any "strong soldiers," so we know right away this is garbage. God has weak vessels who desperately need Him, and the truth is that God does not give us more than we can bear. Ever.

"Money is the root of all evil."

Nope. Sure isn't. *People* are the root of all evil, and the Bible passage that is most falsely accused here is clearly 1 Timothy 6:10, which says "the love of money is a root of all kinds of evil." If anybody has told you this lie, and somehow convinced you that money is bad, that being financially prosperous is bad, or made you feel guilty because you actually have money, they were wrong. Money is a powerful tool. It can be used to help people, to build communities, and to find cures for diseases that save many lives. The problem is not *having money*. The problem is money having *you*.

"All roads lead to Heaven."

If you want to win points and be popular, this is the lie for you. This is the *everybody loves me* lie. Offend no one, please everyone, make friends, and win people. The big problem here is that it's impossible. In every way. It's very trendy right now to say things like this because people believe so many different things.

I heard a politician once thank at least seven faiths and seven Gods of different religions. In his mind, I think he thought this was respectful, and perhaps to some it was. I didn't think so. I would much rather know what he believes, even if it's different from me, because at least he'd be clear. After that prayer, I knew this person would be a less than stellar leader because he "took a little from each." Picture a person tied to four other people, with all four running in different directions. This is not a picture of peace and stability. The lie that "more is better" is epically false, especially when it comes to the matter of spirit and soul.

This lie is so muddled and peddled so frequently that it is confusing people. The truth is that somebody has to be right, and somebody has to be wrong.

"Carl, what's good for you is great. But this works for me. And after all, all roads lead to Heaven. We are headed to the same place."

The person who said this to me was a Buddhist who also wore New Age crystals and had a red Kabbalah bracelet on the hand in which he predictably held his Bible. He once told me, "I'm covering all my bases, spiritually." I respect a lot about this man, but this was a conversation that needed to be had. I told him the truth, which is that Christians and Buddhists and New Age people and those who practice Kabbalah believe completely different definitions of "Heaven," and each "faith" has vastly different views on why we are here and how to treat people. That one fact puts a stop to this entire Ferris wheel of options.

My road as a Christian leads to one place: Jesus. Jesus said He was and is the only road to God and the absolute only hope for humanity—and, one day, Heaven. He said clearly we have all sinned and only He could atone this sinful separation. He represents a direct affront to any other line of thinking. In related news, He was crucified for this. Sometimes, speaking what you believe to be true will cost you.

But Jesus either spoke truth, and He is who He says He is, or He is an outright liar and the most destructive force humanity has ever seen. That's why the other lie that comes in this package—"Jesus was a good teacher, but He was not God"—is explosively wrong. Because we would never call a teacher who convinced millions upon millons of people to forsake everything and follow him to the ends of the Earth because He was God when in fact He wasn't "good." We would call him "psychotic." Jesus forced the issue of truth, for better or for worse, depending on what you believe.

I couldn't let my Buddhist "all faiths" friend continue to think his idea of the afterlife, which includes being reincarnated, is the same as what I believe. And guess what? We are still friends.

This is relevant because at the core of the *everybody loves me* lie is the idea that confrontation, right and wrong, is bad. *That* is a lie. Confrontation is amazing when done right. Challenging our thinking by discussing it in detail should build us all up, not tear us down. In no way am I saying, "I am right." I believe what I believe with my whole heart, and you can hold what you believe near and dear to yours. But the truth is, somebody is wrong. And somebody is right. It's still okay to say that in our modern world, no matter how many people try to say you're intolerant simply because you hold a view.

The whole idea of tolerance is a sham as well. Think about that for a moment: If we must "understand" every single view people hold, how about the guy who says, "My view is that I want your car. Give it to me. It's my belief." No sir, I will not. I will not tolerate your belief even for a second. It's okay to challenge each other, especially with things that have major consequences. Like, you know, *the meaning of life and eternity.*

The lie is that disagreement must breed disconnection and disparagement. That's not always true. And when that does happen, that's called life.

There is a comedian/political commentator named Bill Maher you may have heard of. I find him extremely sharp, generally funny, and his outspokenness gets him in trouble quite frequently. He is a proud atheist and very anti-religion. But I actually appreciate what he says about Christians, and that is simply: "Christians are absolutely crazy to believe what they believe." I appreciate the fact that he keeps it real. I think he is just as crazy for what he believes. I think he's wrong. But at least he's not pulling any punches. I'm secure in my faith, and therefore I don't need to necessarily *defend* myself all the time. I don't see a man like that *attacking* me. Maybe that's the key. I can even learn from and admire some things about a man like that while standing strong on the parts I disagree with.

We can't spend our whole lives building walls in front of those who are not like us and surrounding ourselves with only those who agree with us on every point. Differences lead to discussions. In fact, talking about things that are hard and complicated will eventually create more opportunities and more relationships, because the truth is that everybody is thinking about these things. Some are just better at lying about it.

"God took my loved one because He needed another angel in Heaven."

Maybe you have heard a well-meaning preacher or friend say this to somebody who needed comfort after a very difficult loss. I've heard it said at funerals. I've heard people tell others this lie because they simply don't know what else to say. But this is one of those *good today, bad tomorrow* lies. It might make you feel a little better for a moment, but if this is true, it causes more painful questions down the road. If it is true, this would mean that Heaven has an employment issue. God has apparently run out of staff, so now He is arbitrarily taking people to fill some big-time needs in Heaven.

The truth is that, yes, God is sovereign and can bring good out of anything. But people die sometimes, and it makes no sense. We won't have these answers until the day we enter eternity ourselves. We live in a broken world, with broken people, and the result is that there is sickness and there is death and there are consequences. Bad things happen to good people all the time.

Although it's harder to hear sometimes, it's better to rest in that truth than to take temporary comfort in something that isn't actually true. If you have ever lost somebody and you know that pain, I'm with you. But I would rather take comfort knowing that God can help us live lives that make a difference, and we can keep people's legacies alive even when they are taken too soon.

"You can catch flies with honey, but you can catch way more honeys bein' fly!"

This is, in fact, not a lie at all.

"Speak to the universe, and it will speak back. You get out what you put in."

"What are you doing?"

It was my fair question to a friend who was twirling in the wind, with a cool ocean breeze blowing our way as he breathed heavily in and out and did some funky hand motions.

He said, "I'm speaking to the universe. I'm putting out good vibes. I need them to come back tenfold this week. It's a big week." I told my friend, "Let's go have a coffee. We need to talk. Tell the universe you will be right back."

Believe me when I say my friend is not alone when it comes to oceanside "vibe sending." But here is the bad news to anybody who has been told you can speak to the universe: It's not listening. The universe doesn't have a name. It does not have ears. It does not have a soul. It doesn't bring "good vibes" and does not take appointments. Furthermore, in this life, yes, to a degree, we reap what we sow. If you steal long enough, you will most likely reap jail time at some point. And if you are a genuinely kind and faithful person, you will be far more likely to know people exactly like that because shared values are magnetic and contagious.

But to a much larger degree, this life can never be about doing things to get more in return. Because that would be cosmically uneven. There are amazing people in this world who help others, give all they have, open up their lives and homes to those in need, and spend every waking hour doing what they can to make our world better. And they would not have "anything to show for it" according to our world's standards. Conversely, we all know people who are the opposite of what I just described, and they seem to have a lot. Of everything. They don't "deserve it." They didn't "earn it." Maybe they even just got lucky. The truth is that the rewards in this life are truly much deeper than what we would call "success." You can't count changed lives. You can't get awards for changing somebody's day. And you can't always quantify lifting the burden of another life. The truth is that sometimes we are going to do what's right and in return receive what's wrong. This puts the emphasis on the "why" we do what we do in the first place.

I talked to a guy who said, "I'm not getting paid what I deserve. Do you feel like you get paid what you deserve?" My honest answer was my prayer that no job in this life can pay me what I deserve because I want to do so much and give so much more than what is required. I'm an impossible hire. I'm thankful to breathe. I'm grateful to wake up daily and do what I can to get better. And therefore I'm never frustrated, because I never bought the *I deserve this and more lie* in the first place.

Sure, it's perfectly okay to have high standards and earn a living in this life you are proud of. But my rewards? You can't count them. Sometimes you can't see them. So the truth I live by is that I am going to focus on the "give." Others can have all the "give and take" they want, but I will pass. I want to be the kind of friend who is giving and not looking for the return all the time. Because I have already moved on to the next thing I want to give. It's a very powerful way to live. When you are beholden to no man, no job, no "ceiling"—none of those things can dictate your happiness or worth. That's the truth.

And in regard to the universe, I expect nothing from it, because it's not a "thing." It's never going to call you back. In fact, it doesn't care about me or you. However, you can speak to the *creator* of the universe, and that is a much more fulfilling fact. I don't want to waste any time in this life expecting the wrong things because I was told the wrong things and I believed them.

"You can't trust people. People will hurt you."

We see this—what I call the *once and for all* lie—all over the place in different scenarios. It can even morph into things like, "You can't trust men." Or, "You must keep your guard up." Or, "Don't let people get too close." These are lies. The truth, and even the shred of truth in some of these statements, is that, yes, people can hurt you. Some men (and women) do lie. It is wise to use wisdom and be guarded. To keep some people at a safe distance.

The key word here is *some*. Separating an incident from becoming a life theme is important. Especially when we have been wounded or let down by people. But this lie can tempt people to go through something and say, "Never again. Once and for all, I'm done with that." Those words are music to my ears in some areas. But not when it comes to people.

This lie will keep you out of love, out of hope, out of relationships that matter.

We have to learn how to fix a factor in the equation without blowing up the concept of "math." Nobody would go to a restaurant and have a bad experience and say, "A'ight. No more food for me, *ever*." Food is not the issue. Where you pick to eat the food is. Wisdom destroys this lie. Don't allow what may be legitimately painful parts of your life to set the tone for the rest of it.

If I have not convinced you yet, I heard a teenager say, "Oh well, I don't plan on getting married. You can't trust people these days."

I said, "Who told you that?" She said, "My mom did." Some lies not only destroy you, but they get a good shot at destroying the generations behind you.

"God helps those who help themselves."

Just no. In totality.

If we could "help ourselves," we would. Jesus said, "Blessed are those who are at the end of their rope. With less of you, there is more of God and His rule." The truth is that self-help is limited help. I'm glad we have options.

These are just some common lies I hear enough to know that people really believe unhealthy things. But if we can at minimum take a long look at what we believe or have believed our whole lives, we can start to find out some cracks in our own life foundation and start to rebuild and remodel where necessary.

Sometimes it can happen quick. I remember talking to a fellow dad once whose daughter said something that was crazy. It was along the lines of, "Truck that, Dad. I'll do what I want."

My friend said, "Oh, get ready for that. Teenage girls just say what they want. It's what happens when they get older."

I looked at him and said very calmly, "Maybe on the planet you live on." I told him how, in fact, that is a lie. Some parents are just lazy, and over time, as they let their children push more and more boundaries, they get out of control. But we don't have to accept that. When teenagers lash out, often there is a really obvious reason—if parents can explore, investigate, and be present long enough to find out what's happening.

My friend heard me loud and clear, and sure enough he set some new boundaries for his daughter. He stopped believing the *kids do this* lie, and she stopped functioning under that lie that was by default handed down to her.

If you look at different areas of your life that cause frustration, you are going to find a lie hiding in plain sight somewhere. And you can either confront it now, while there is still time, or you can let it ride. Thing is, it's not riding. It's *driving*. I propose you take the keys back and make sure that truth is your navigational go-to, not something that should never have been in your system to begin with.

It can take some time. And often some tears. But it's worth it to take this journey. Even if it takes you so far back you realized the lies began to draw lines before you knew what hit you.

I read an article not long ago that ruined my day. An FBI team raided a house when they got a tip about where a girl who had been kidnapped, missing for over two years, was being held. When they stormed the house, they found the girl in squalid conditions, in a trancelike state. A trauma unit and team of doctors began to take care of the girl and attend to her needs, and they asked her what her name was.

She said, "My name is Idiot."

The lead investigator asked her again, and she answered the same way. The agent then said, "Honey, why do you think your name is Idiot?"

She said softly, "Because that's what they call me. That's my name."

She was seven years old. For her entire time in captivity, she was called a lie. Just long enough for her to believe it.

I'm praying for that little girl, wherever she is, every day—that truth will win out, and God can somehow repair the evil intent and damage done to her little soul.

Perhaps your story doesn't seem as dramatic or heart-wrenching. But if you have ever heard something or built your life on something that is not true, maybe this moment can be that FBI raid to your soul. There is still time for all of us to repair some broken things.

An English teacher once told me that I couldn't concentrate long enough to write anything of worth. That was a lie, and I'm going to send her my book. Maybe somebody told you that you were an accident. Maybe in your parents' minds but not in God's eyes. He made you. He knew you were coming. Believe that truth. Perhaps on the outside today people think you are doing pretty good. And maybe you are. But if you harbor a lie and it's still affecting you, "pretty good" isn't good enough. You are worth greatness. Not just survival.

In my life, I have a no-tolerance policy for lies—including lies that I want to believe about myself sometimes. It happens to us all. I'm just glad I was told the truth: What others say about me or have said about me or will say about me matters. Words carry weight. But they don't matter as much as the words *I* say about me. Those hold the most weight.

own the chapter

The truth will set you free. To live in real, Godly truth, there can be no mixture. You can't have mostly truth with a little bit of lie involved in any area, and then expect that to work in any way. I used to love a TV show called *Pimp My Ride*. It was a show where people would take really average cars and have them extremely modified, fixed up and painted differently. I always found it funny, because no matter how somebody would try to dress up their Honda Accord, it was always still a Honda Accord. A fancy lie is still a lie. A lie you have learned to live with and function with; although you are surviving, you are in no way thriving like you could be. Truth forces complete and total change. It may be unsettling at first, but building your life on what is true, what is right? Ends up creating a life you don't have to "dress up or modify." You will be excited to let it stand out on its own. Build your life, one truth at a time.

Chapter Twenty-Eight

You Don't Need to Save the World

WHEN THERE IS A GIANT void of anything, even a small amount of that which is missing is that much more significant. This is really good news for those of us who turn on the TV or open up the newspaper and see so much pain—who look at the problems we face in our world and feel discouraged due to the seemingly insurmountable odds we face to bring change. Make no mistake, the need is great. But I believe our opportunity is greater.

Nobody appreciates a flashlight until they are lost, it's dark, and they have no way out. We can be those flashlights, and if you get enough flashlights working at the same time, a dark room can light up quick. The key to this thought being a reality, though, is people understanding that you have to activate what you have. If we refuse to do this, we also eliminate our right to criticize, complain, or whine/blog/tweet about whatever it is we don't like.

We have a saying at our church that goes like this: "If you ain't helping, you ain't helping. And if you're not helping, I don't want to hear you talking." This means I'm not interested in the criticism of our world, our church, our politics, if you have no blood on your hands. If you are in the fight? I want to hear what you have to say. But if I did not see you on the battlefield, I do not want to see you afterward to hear about what I could have done better.

The temptation to be a spectator is real. In fact, it's easier than ever. I read one day about "bystander syndrome" in an article about a young girl who was raped outside her high-school prom. That alone is horrific. What makes it heartbreaking and evil is that police say at least forty people saw this happening and passed by. This girl was brutalized for over three hours. People saw it happening. Maybe they were scared, maybe they didn't know what to do, but the fact remains that they did nothing.

Psychologists say that it's an actual condition, where the presence of many spectators freezes people. It's almost like there is safety in numbers, thus people do nothing. I'm not an avid reader of WorldStarHipHop and this is not intended as a disparaging dig at the blog. But the facts are that websites like it and many, many others will post videos of fights and other atrocious things, and people watch these videos. In the *millions*. I clicked on one and was sick to my stomach within seconds. It was a high-school fight, and there were dozens of people watching and filming. That was bad enough. But when I saw the actual viewer count of the video is when I realized yet again there is a whole lot of good to be done in this world. And the standard for acceptable living and human decency is so low that if we can show even a fraction more kindness, mercy, hope, and encouragement, we can keep turning the tide.

When we first landed in NYC, a few people asked me if it was overwhelming—the sheer size of the city, the overt need, the cultural melting pot that is the city that never sleeps. All real factors to be sure. I was asked, "Are you guys gonna reach a city of millions?"

I said, "I'm not worried about the millions. I'm worried about the *ones*. As in each one. One by one."

I have never stopped thinking like that.

I've shared with our church an account in the Bible that I'll share with you now. It shows what a little bit of effort and determination can do. Basically, Jesus was healing people and word was getting out. The Bible says Jesus began to preach and heal, and so many people came that they couldn't fit anybody else in. You can imagine the scene. Blind people, people with leprosy, the destitute and the desperate, vying to get in the presence of somebody, anybody, who could help them.

We then find out that a group of four men had brought their friend, who had been lame since birth, on his mat. They couldn't get in, but that was just the beginning. These four men must have thought this was their one chance to help their friend, and they were out of options. So they improvised. They got on the roof of the meetinghouse where Jesus was speaking below, then they carved a hole in the roof and lowered the man down directly in front of Jesus. Jesus looked at this man, and He healed him. The guy got up, grabbed his mat, and we can safely assume he high-stepped out of the meeting like Deion Sanders returning a punt. High-stepping so everybody knew he'd scored, big time.

But my favorite part of the story isn't even that. It's the guys who made it possible for their friend to be in the position to get healed. There were four of them, and I always imagine them to be four New Yorkers. One would have been the classic brash New Yorker, who just yells the obvious: "We can't get in! And I'm not happy about it!" The second guy would have been like a tech guy with a pocket protector who comes up with plans: "We need to carve a hole. We will need a saw, and most likely a rope." The third guy would have been the shifty Brooklyn guy who "knows a guy": "We need a rope? Cool. I know a guy from Long Island who knows a guy on Canal Street who sells rope on the cheap. I got this. Fahhhhh-getaboutit." The fourth guy? The rich New Yorker: "Good plan, guys. Make the deal, send me the check. Because I got money." And together, they all did something. Not everything. But together they played their parts perfectly, and forever they would have talked about their friend, who came in lying down, was face-to-face with the living Messiah, and walked out of that same meeting.

What's vital to this event in history is what was *not* recorded in the account. Mainly, the names of the four men. We don't ever find out who they were, what they did, or what they achieved after this epic moment. All we know is what the Bible says:

It says, "Some men came."

Some men. Maybe the story of our world getting better won't be about a megastar. Maybe the history books will record that "New York City and beyond defied all logic and started a new trend of love and peace in the face of war and hate. We didn't get any names, but there were a lot of them. They gave, they loved, they sacrificed. And the result is all we have the details for."

I have made peace with that ending. Sometimes the

spotlight will shine on us, and sometimes the shadows of life will consume us. We don't have much control over that. All we can do is make sure we are doing the same thing, no matter what. Doing what we can, while we can. Not for credit, not for fame, not for money, not for popularity. In fact, true change often comes at the expense of one or all of those things.

But I know one thing: We can't do *nothing*.

The opportunity is too great and the need is too urgent.

I will end this book where my calling truly began in earnest. The calling to help anybody and everybody I have a chance to help. Ready or not, equipped or not, my calling is to do *something*. And one sentence started that fire in my soul.

I was at a church conference of about thirty thousand people in a giant arena. By this point, I was all in on my faith. I was proactive. I was passionate. But I'm not sure I was reckless in my pursuit. Meaning I still overthought some moments I should have owned. Maybe I was scared to talk to a stranger. Maybe I preached a point with some hesitation rather than outright, vein-popping conviction.

On this night I had a friend with me who had just gotten out of drug rehab. His life was painful from the time he could remember. Sexually abused by a family member as a little boy.

Bounced around from one unstable condition to the next. Into drugs at an age where boys should be into sports and possibly girls. The road led eventually to heroin, and by God's grace somebody loved him enough to drag him to rehab where he began the long journey back to real life.

At one point during a really powerful song, I looked around this arena full of people singing. One song. What seemed like one voice, although thousands made it up. I turned to my friend to say, "Isn't this awesome?" But he was sitting down with his face in his hands, quietly sobbing. I put my arm around him to comfort him, and had no idea that his next sentence would sear my soul to its core.

I said, "What's wrong? What's going through your mind?"

He said, "I wish that SOMEBODY. WOULD. HAVE. TOLD. ME. SOONER. I see all these people, singing so loud, talking about Jesus, looking so happy. Nobody ever told me nothing. And I would have listened! I was searching my whole life! I'm glad I'm here now. I'm glad God didn't give up on me. But I wasted so many years. I've been through so much pain. I just wish somebody would have told me sooner."

I didn't have any words that night. I remember my own hands covering my own face as I couldn't control my own tears that were falling. I thought about how many people would probably express that same feeling. How many people had I walked by in my life? How many times had I been so consumed with my issues that I forgot that *surely* somebody in my life had it worse, and I could help them?

I prayed that night something that I remember was more a vow than a prayer. I told God that I was sorry for missing so many moments. And I promised that now and forever I will be a "somebody" who He could use to reach "anybody." Rich and famous. Broke and faceless. The down and out. The up and out.

"God, will you use me to help people know sooner?"

Since that day? I have not done all the right things. Far from it. I have not saved the world, not even close. But I have done my best to be available and to be relentless. I cannot express how much joy there is in doing simply what you can. My prayer for you is that you will be stirred to do something.

I can't promise that people will know your name. I can't promise that the rain in life is not going to fall on your face from time to time. It will. But I think the option to own the moment is so good that when the rain does fall? You might smile about it. After all, what other option do you have? I choose to be a part of this plan: that we don't have to accept what we see. We can change it. And that is good enough for me.

I found myself walking down 34th Street the other day, thinking and praying as I do. Sometimes in NYC, random famous people will walk around, and tourists are on high alert so they can take pictures that nobody cares about. As I walked by, a woman hopped excitedly off a bench with her camera and shouted, "Hey! Hey you! Are you . . . somebody? Can I take a picture with you? You look like somebody. I can't place the name, though . . ."

I assured her that, yes, I was "somebody"—Carl from Virginia Beach, Virginia—but not in the way she was asking, and she should save that camera battery for a real star. It was awesome. I pointed to a café around the corner that famous people actually frequent and said, "Head over there, and I'm sure you will find what you're looking for. If you do see a famous person, make sure you put your flash on extra bright and shine it in their eyes. They love that."

She said, "Thank you! I knew I would find somebody in this city to point me in the right direction."

She seemed happy. Sometimes being a "somebody" is quite all right. Especially if it means somebody else gets to have a brighter day.

Even if it's just for a moment.

own the chapter

We have made bringing change to our world so complex that many people never even try. And yes, the problems we face are huge, but the steps and the moments we need to take to get there are small, they are frequent, and they are available for anybody who is willing to take small steps that will lead to major significance someday. What will be the one thing you will do today that could make a huge difference in the life of another? If you leave it to "just happen," I have found that it actually rarely ever happens. Conversely, if you prepare to be a blessing to others I have found that it leads to a road where you end up doing more than you set out to do. If you woke up tomorrow and decided to "own a moment," literally a single act of kindness and thoughtfulness toward another, I believe the impact on your life will be significant. We have all heard people tell a story, and they say, "Well, you know. One thing led to another." You can't have the latter without the former. Doing everything? Impossible. Doing something is completely reasonable. Create moments. Own moments. Remember moments. We don't get a second shot at this life, and my prayer for you is that you would never underestimate the power of the moments you control. I have endeavored to live my life in such a way where I rarely have to say, "I missed it." I want to be able to say, "I owned it. I made the most of it." The best part of your story has yet to be written. Make sure you write it, with passion and purpose.

Acknowledgments

THANK YOU, STEVE AND CATHY LENTZ, for being my heroes, my mentors, my friends, and my gold standard for everything in this life. Dad, the highest compliment somebody can pay me is when they say, "You remind me of your dad." I don't hear it enough yet, but someday if that's the most frequent way I am described by those who are my friends, I will have done well in this life. You have more integrity and kindness than any man I have ever known, and I'm proud to be your son. Mom, I have never had to wonder what a strong, Godly woman looks like because I have gotten to watch your life my whole life. I love you and I'm thankful that I get to be your son.

Thank you to my sisters, Mary, Bethany, and Corrie. All

three of you have loved me exactly the same through every random stage of my random life. Unconditionally. I'm certain that I would not be in a position to love Jesus like I do—let alone write a book—without your constant love in my life.

Thank you, Kevin and Marilyn Brett, for being so loving, so kind, and so trusting. To be husband to your beloved daughter is the highest honor for me, and I promise I will never stop trying to become a better man, and a better support to her. I love you both and respect you greatly. Thanks for taking a chance on me.

Thank you, Brian and Bobbie Houston, for giving Laura and me an opportunity to serve people in our amazing church. I have never known people who are as passionate about seeing other people win and thrive and move forward as you two are. I am one of the many who have simply walked into a place of blessing and influence that you opened up so generously. Thanks for taking risks on people like me.

Thank you, Steve Kelly, for seeing a young guy in church who absolutely did not feel like he belonged, and taking me to lunch. Thanks for speaking about Jesus so powerfully that I made a real decision to follow him after hearing you talk about the love of God. Thanks for pointing me the right way in ministry. I am forever grateful for your investment in my life.

Thank you, Jan Miller and Nena Madonia, for convincing me that I should do this book. Both of you have been so kind, so helpful, so expert at what you do that you left me no choice! I love you both, and I'm thankful I get to share this vulnerable book journey with you both.

Thank you, Jon Karp and Sean Manning, for your patience and your belief in this endeavor. "On paper" our paths probably would not have crossed naturally. I think it's special that they did anyway and the result has ended up "on paper." Jon, you have given a lot of room for me to find my "voice" as a writer, and it's still a giant work in progress. But I am so glad it has begun, with your wisdom and help throughout. Sean, you are a phenomenal editor, and the fact you didn't go crazy trying to figure out how to work with me is a testament to your gifting and temperament. You have taught me so much and should this book help anybody, you had a massive hand in it. Thank you for working so hard on this with me.

To Hillsong NYC: There are no words to express the honor it is to pastor a church like we have. The most amazing people on Earth can be found wherever our church meets. It's been said that "We become like those we hang out with." I am becoming a better man daily due to the privilege I have to be around and serve with people who give so much, love others so relentlessly, and refuse to accept what has been so we can pursue what can be. "Church in the wild" for life. I love you with all my heart!

About the Author

CARL LENTZ pastors Hillsong Church NYC, a thriving Christian congregation with locations in Manhattan and New Jersey. Born the youngest of four in Williamsburg, Virginia, he was raised in a Christian household but struggled to connect with the local church concept and religion in general. At age twenty, he discovered his calling and enrolled in the Hillsong College in Australia, where the Hillsong Church was founded in 1983. While completing his pastoral training there, Lentz met his wife and co-pastor, Laura. In 2010, they helped launch Hillsong Church NYC, the first U.S.-based branch and one of the fastest-growing churches in America. Known for reaching "the famous to the nameless," the couple now lives in Montclair, New Jersey, with their three amazing children. *Own The Moment* is his first book.